Learning to Learn Accountancy

First edition July 2002
Reprinted in January 2003

ISBN 0 7517 1063 6

British Library Cataloguing-in-Publication Data
A catalogue record for this book is available from the British Library

Published by

BPP Professional Education
Aldine House, Aldine Place
London W12 8AW

www.bpp.com

Printed in Great Britain by

Ashford Colour Press
Unit 600
Fareham Reach
Fareham Road
Gosport
Hants PO13 0FW

All our rights reserved. No part of this publication may be reproduced, stored in a retrieval system or transmitted, in any form or by any means, electronic, mechanical, photocopying, recording or otherwise, without the prior written permission of BPP Professional Education.

Contents

Preface

Learning styles — 1

Types of subject — 25

Study environment — 41

Study skills — 63

Revision — 91

Types of question — 107

Exam paper — 139

Preface

Preface

Learning accountancy

You've committed yourself to *passing* your accountancy exams. However you *may* not be completely clear yet about *what* you'll be studying. You've studied before of course, at school certainly, at university perhaps. You know studying accountancy will be a bit different, but how different?

Knowledge and skills

Accountancy exams will *give you* the *knowledge and skills* you need to occupy a senior position in the workplace.

Accountancy qualifications are designed to be broad-based, giving you the opportunity to work in a variety of different environments. To qualify, you thus need knowledge of a variety of subjects.

Accountancy exams also test ways in which you *use your knowledge*. This means *applying what you know* to *solving problems* and *communicating* your solutions *clearly*.

Time

One other concern you may have is the time available for study. The first exams may be six months rather than two years away. You have more commitments now than you ever had before.

The description we've given of studying for accountancy exams may have raised a number of questions in your mind.

Well that's a start. One thing we want you to do throughout your studies is to think constantly about **how** *you're learning and* **what** *you're learning.*

What we've done on the next couple of pages is ask a BPP author some questions about how she learned accountancy. We suggest that you try to answer the questions in relation to exams that you've previously taken.

- *If you struggle with any of the questions,* **don't worry***; this book will give you the answers.*
- *If you don't understand why the questions are significant,* **don't worry***; this book will explain their importance.*
- *If you feel that the questions have highlighted weaknesses in what you've done before,* **don't worry***; this book will help you eliminate those weaknesses.*

In this book we're going to show you how you can learn accountancy

- ▶ **Efficiently** We don't want you to spend unnecessary time studying.
- ▶ **Effectively** We do want you to pass your exams.

Questions

Q1 — Did you do any preparation before you embarked upon learning accountancy?

No, not really. My training college sent me a little workbook on basic bookkeeping, which I worked through for a couple of hours, but nothing other than that.
However, I did have to do a basic maths revision day later on in my course, when it became obvious that GCSE was a distant memory…

Q2 — Did you know about learning styles, or have any idea what your strengths/weaknesses were in this area?

I didn't know anything about different intelligences etc. However, I was aware that I was a more 'wordy' than 'numbery' person, if you know what I mean. I did history at university - I hadn't done any maths for years.

Q3 — So, had you studied any of the subjects you faced in your accountancy exams before?

Not at all. I thought about doing Economics A level, but chose Latin instead. That was really helpful when it came to accountancy, you can imagine! Well, except on some of the law papers. It was all really new to me. Some of it felt like a different language.

Q4 — Did you find you had any subject preferences?

Unsurprisingly I suppose, given what I've said about being wordy, I showed a clear preference in my first year for law and management. But I also surprised myself by finding economics interesting - I'd thought that I'd find it really hard.

Q5 — What study method did you use?

My firm chose the 'link' method for me, which meant that I attended training college for a series of single weeks.

Q6 — When did you study privately?

In my first year, it seemed like all the time! All the subjects were new, and I found that it took me a long time to understand everything. As I got more familiar with the subjects, I found I could use my time more effectively. I tended to work in the evenings and early mornings round my lectures. When not at college I found it easier to study early before I went to work than trying to do it after a whole day at work - but that is just me, I'm a morning person.

Q7 — Where did you study?

In the course of three years, lots of places. In my first year I worked in my bedroom while living in someone else's house. In my second year, I got my own place and worked in the living room. I often went into college early to run through my notes and do question practice. I sometimes worked in the office in the mornings or the library. I did a lot of revision on the bus as well.

Q8 — Did you plan your own work?

Yes, within the boundaries of the homework given to me by my tutors. I used to set up general plans for the weeks between attending college and I particularly used to plan revision, before I went on the revision course at the college. That way I knew that I had reviewed things I found difficult before it was revised in class.

Q9 How much study did you used to do?

It really depended on circumstances. Between visits to college I used to try and work on the principle of doing an hour in the morning where possible, and perhaps an hour plus in the evening at minimum. If I missed one day, I'd try to catch up on another. Sometimes however there were weeks where I was working overtime or travelling a long way, and it wasn't really viable to study before and after, so I didn't. And once in a while it was good to consciously take a break. I always tried to keep at least one day at the weekend 'study free', but it wasn't always possible, especially close to the exams.

Q10 How did you find lectures?

It soon became apparent that I am not a very aural learner. I found it difficult to concentrate on what was said, and found that I had to take notes of what the lecturer was saying to focus on it. Once I had got to grips with listening, it was good to be talked through things in a simple, clear way.

Q11 What was your favourite 'study skill'?

Notetaking. I made copious notes (on lectures, textbooks, questions ...). I found that the act of writing stuff helped me to remember it, and trying to put it into my own words helped me to understand it better.

Q12 Do you have a favourite revision tip?

I have two favourite techniques - posters and index cards (now, of course, I write passcards for other people!). Index cards have seen me through Uni and accountancy now. I think I must have an A5 shaped brain! But just because I like them doesn't mean everyone else will. Revision is a very individual thing.

Q13 What sort of time scale did you set on revising?

I tried to make sure that I had a handle on everything before I went on my revision course, so that it genuinely was revision. Sometimes that meant revising things from early in the teaching course just before revision started. Generally though I set myself up a revision timetable from day one of the revision course - dovetailing with my tutor's recommendations when it was right for me.

Q14 Did you do question practice?

Yes. Basically I am a swot and I mainly do what people tell me to do! Particularly on the 'numbery' papers, especially financial accounting, I found that it was the only way to get my approach right and eliminate silly errors. I have to admit on 'wordy' papers I sometimes restricted myself to an answer plan, because I was fairly convinced that my essay style was okay.

Q15 Did you get things marked?

Yes. Course exams and mocks were always marked.

Q16 How did you approach exam day?

Unfortunately I am dreadful at exams. I get unfeasibly nervous about going into exam halls. So you would have found me outside, taking really deep breaths and trying not to be sick, trying to relax. Not the best start! Once I got in there, I knew I had to concentrate on exam technique so I was really strict about timings on questions. Practising in exam conditions is a real help for that.

How this book can help you

How BPP can help you

Our team is made up of qualified accountants who *know* what you're facing. *We* can *help you* through the challenges because we've been through them ourselves. *We can help you succeed.*

We never forget that you are an *individual*. We appreciate that you will find some subjects more demanding than others. We realise that your study patterns will differ from other students'.

The services and products we provide are there to meet *your* needs. You can *rely* on them from the start of your studies to your last exam.

- Published products
- Home study
- Computer based learning
- Classroom courses

BPP - WE'RE HERE FOR YOU

How you study

We shall show you how to understand and remember the material you learn. We shall challenge you to assess where your strengths lie, and also how to find out where you need to do most work.

We shall also discuss organising your studies, particularly during the critical period in the run up to the exams. And as for the exams - we'll show you how to approach those as well.

Where and when you study

We shall be looking at the environment in which you study; studying in the right place with the right atmosphere can enhance the effectiveness and efficiency of your study. As you have limited time, we shall also discuss when to study and how much to do.

What you study

We shall provide a brief introduction to the most important subjects that you will meet. We also cover the key skills you need to pass - most importantly how to approach the different types of question that you will encounter.

We suggest • • •

that you read this book from cover to cover first of all to see what it can offer you. Then throughout your studies you can dip in and out of it depending on what assistance you need at any one time.

Learning styles

Introduction

This book aims to help you to be proactive in your accountancy studies. It is not about learning accountancy. It is about learning to learn accountancy.

Learning is often something that people fear, particularly if it is something they have chosen to study while trying to carry out a full-time job as well.

In this Chapter, we will explore some features of learning that you may not have considered before. There are a number of different methods of learning; we shall investigate which suits you best. Then in further chapters we shall focus on different methods of

▶ Obtaining knowledge
▶ Answering questions
▶ Facing exams

We shall try and look at the best way for YOU to do each of these things, based on what we discover in this Chapter about how YOU learn best.

Let's have a look at two definitions which will be important to use in the course of understanding this book.

Learn — To obtain knowledge of facts or of how to do things, or an understanding of ideas.

Teach — To give knowledge

There is a difference being taught and learning. Being taught is a passive thing, and we want it to be a proactive thing, and we want you to be proactive in your studies.

It is in the nature of a gift that you do not have to (or may feel unable to) accept something that is given to you.

This book aims to help you to make the effective link between the gift, and acceptance of the knowledge.

You may find that you agree with Festus, who said in c59 AD:

> "... much learning doth make thee mad."

We hope that after reading this book, you'll have **changed your mind**.

Lectures

> *Have you ever sat in a lecture, and found that the lecturer's voice is very soporific, the room seems to be getting warmer, and your mind wanders to any and every subject under the sun except the task in hand and the content of the lecture?*
>
> The lecturer is talking with more and more emphasis, and waving her hands around a little, scribbling earnestly on the overhead projector screen. It is clear that this is the most important part of the lecture to this point, but all you can picture is what Mars might look like. The classroom is beginning to feel weightless, and all your classmates are beginning to look a little green…
>
> *"Such labour'd nothings, in so strange a style, amaze th' unlearned, and make the learned smile."*
>
> Alexander Pope

Accountancy is commonly taught aurally, that is, in lecture theatres at professional training centres or colleges.

You may be booked onto a course at a BPP centre, either to study for an extended period on release from work, or intermittently or in the evenings.

Lectures are a very effective way for people who have knowledge to give that knowledge to a group of people at the same time. For your employers, it is also an economically sound method: to engage individual tutors for each of you would probably be cost-prohibitive.

However, most people have an experience similar to 'the Martian experience' (outlined to the left) in their studies, some have them more than others. A key part of turning teaching into learning will be to identify how you respond to lectures, and putting plans into action to convert the teaching you receive into learning.

IDENTIFY how you respond to lectures

DEVELOP action plans

IMPLEMENT the plans & start **LEARNING**

Converting **teaching** • • •

'…and you should consolidate these accounts…'

'…what have I got for dinner…'

Home study

Another common way of studying for accountancy is to undertake a course of Home Study. You may be enrolled on a BPP Home Study course.

Of course, even if you are not enrolled on such a course, taking any kind of accountancy training will involve you studying some part of your course at home in the form of homework from lectures, or your own development of what you have been taught - your own personal learning.

A BPP Study Text in some ways acts a personal trainer. The author is giving you knowledge through the pages. If you are on a BPP Home Study programme, you are also offered a tailored study plan of how to approach the textbook and practice questions, and on-line support.

Studying on your own can lead to those dramatic, head-exploding moments (outlined to the right) from time to time. In order to learn accountancy effectively by this method you need also to identify how you approach such learning and then put an effective study system into place, using all the elements made available to you.

> *...Alternatively this may be your experience...*
>
> *You've been in the library for two hours. You have your BPP Study Text open before you, and have read page 12 three times. You could now recite the titles, authors and publishers of the row of books in front of you in the correct order and win millions on a quiz show, but couldn't tell anyone how to fill in their personal tax return for love nor money.*
>
> *The skin on your head is feeling a bit tight. As the seconds tick by, you can feel it getting tighter and tighter, until your head explodes. Here endeth the problem...*
>
> *"Books cannot always please, however good. Minds are not always craving for their food."*
>
> *George Crabbey*

• • • into **learning!**

Learning styles questionnaire

Over the following few pages, we shall be trying to assess what types of intelligence you exhibit more strongly and prefer to use. There are two illustrations for you to work through.

Learning styles identification, Illustration 1

Please work through the following questionnaire and tick the boxes **where you agree with the statement.**

Do not think too hard about your answers. This questionnaire consists of 70 questions, but should take you no more than about 5 minutes to answer.

Learning styles questionnaire guidance

Do you agree with the statement? Answering yes or no . . .

If your answer is	ALWAYS	Answer 'yes'	⇒	tick the box
If your answer is	USUALLY	Answer 'yes'	⇒	tick the box
If your answer is	SOMETIMES	Answer 'yes'	⇒	tick the box
If your answer is	SOMETIMES (rarely)	Answer 'no'	⇒	do nothing
If your answer is	NEVER	Answer 'no'	⇒	do nothing

Please work through the illustrations **honestly**.

If you do not, the study systems we guide you towards later in the book will not necessarily be effective for you.

But **don't think too hard** about this questionnaire – give us your **gut answer**.

Questionnaire

1. I love words ☐
2. I love rhythm ☐
3. I picture things ☐
4. I am 'a doer' ☐
5. I like to follow a 'step approach' to complete a task ☐
6. I think actions speak louder than words ☐
7. I find it easy to explain things to other people ☐
8. I like to mull things over in my head ☐
9. I make lists ☐
10. I like to take a moment to order my thoughts ☐
11. My doodles are predominately made of words ☐
12. I am good with my hands ☐
13. I find myself singing advert jingles ☐
14. My doodles are predominately made of pictures or symbols ☐
15. I love chess (the game) ☐
16. I discuss something with others to work out what it means ☐
17. I like to work something out for myself ☐
18. I always go for logic puzzles ☐
19. I will more easily understand how to do something if I do ☐
20. I like riddles ☐
21. If I was going grocery shopping I would make a list ☐
22. If I was going grocery shopping I would visualise me, or someone else, cooking, and the ingredients they would need ☐
23. If I was going grocery shopping I would tell someone what I wanted to buy and take that person with me ☐
24. If I was going grocery shopping I would organise my shopping list so it correlated to the shop layout ☐
25. When someone sings a nursery rhyme I see the characters in my head ☐
26. I could hum three nursery rhymes if you asked me to ☐
27. I choose birthday cards primarily because of the message in the words ☐

(cont)

28	I choose birthday cards primarily because of the picture on the front	☐
29	I would like to send a gorilla-gram in place of a card	☐
30	If I was planning a ski trip I would read a book about skiing	☐
31	I think that I would enjoy skiing	☐
32	If I was planning a ski trip I would look at maps and pictures of the pistes	☐
33	If I was planning a ski trip I would talk to someone who can ski	☐
34	If I was planning a ski trip I would visit a snow-dome	☐
35	I think that I would probably hate skiing	☐
36	If I was planning a ski trip I would starting hearing the Ski Sunday music in my head	☐
37	I like big groups of people	☐
38	I can spend hours talking on the phone	☐
39	I like to meet my friends in groups	☐
40	I like to see my friends on a one-to-one basis, or in smaller groups	☐
41	I have strong opinions	☐
42	People value my opinions and tell me so	☐
43	If I want to remember things I write them down	☐
44	If I want to remember things I repeat them to myself over and over again	☐
45	If I want to remember things I set them to tunes in my head	☐
46	If I want to remember things I attach numbers to them to make it easier	☐
47	I recall things by counting them off on my fingers	☐
48	If I want to remember things I picture them	☐
49	I stay behind after lectures and ask questions if I don't understand	☐
50	I ask questions in class	☐
51	I like to ask the next day when I have had time to think about it	☐
52	If writing an essay, I find it easy to put my thoughts in order	☐
53	I like to draw up an essay plan	☐
54	I prefer to be given a diagram than a page of text	☐
55	I can always calculate the score gained in darts easily	☐

(cont)

56	I have a favourite song	☐
57	I use my hands a lot when I speak	☐
58	I would like a small wedding with close friends and family attending	☐
59	I enjoy team games	☐
60	I enjoy 'Pictionary'	☐
61	I play a musical instrument, or the spoons, pots and pans, or anything…	☐
62	I am the navigator in the family	☐
63	If I was having a dinner-party, I would like to draw up a seating plan	☐
64	I would like to try rock climbing	☐
65	I am good at 'Name that tune'	☐
66	People notice that I am well co-ordinated	☐
67	I enjoy word games such as 'Taboo' and 'Articulate'	☐
68	I am a champion 'Twister' player	☐
69	I always take charge of tuning the radio in	☐
70	I prefer a game like Solitare to a group game	☐

Before you turn to find the 'answers' of this questionnaire, please take time to work through illustration 2 (on the next page).

This is probably a good time to note, however, that there are no right answers to this questionnaire.

It is an observation of how you think, not a test.

Therefore when you do turn to the answers, the number of boxes you tick off does not matter. The 'answer' will lie in ratio of answers you have given, not the absolute answers.

Therefore • • •

DO NOT cast your eye back over this questionnaire and think - 'I haven't answered very many' or 'I've answered too many' and be tempted to amend your answers.

The number of statements identified with is irrelevant. Honestly - there are no high or low scores. You will use your answers only to compare with your own answers.

Learning styles identification, Illustration 2

In the blank page given above please put down all your thoughts about Elephants.

Again: Do not think too hard about this task.
Just do it!

You can take as long as you like over this task.

The seven intelligences

If asked to describe intelligence, you might have referred to really clever people, people who like books, who went to University to read a specialist subject, or something along those lines.

Or you may already be aware of the fact that it is now generally accepted that people have a variety of intelligences, or ways in which they learn. Traditionally learning through our linguistic intelligence has been focused on, now there are seven different areas to focus learning in.

You might think that this is terrifying:

> "Seven ways of learning! I find the one I've got difficult enough…"

But as we shall see in the following pages, this is good news. Learning can be tailored to the way you think - not the other way around.

The boxes on the right are going to summarise the results of your questionnaire (illustration 1).

Linguistic — Total
1, 9, 11, 20, 21, 27, 30, 38, 43, 67

Maths logical
5, 15, 18, 24, 46, 47, 52, 53, 55, 63

Spatial visual
3, 14, 22, 25, 28, 32, 48, 54, 60, 62

Musical
2, 13, 26, 29, 36, 45, 56, 61, 65, 69

Bodily kinaesthetic
4, 6, 12, 19, 31, 34, 57, 64, 66, 68

Interpersonal
7, 16, 23, 33, 37, 39, 42, 49, 50, 59

Intra-personal
8, 10, 17, 35, 40, 41, 44, 51, 58, 70

Analysing the results, Illustration 1

Tick the boxes above that are attached to the numbers of the statements you agreed with in the questionnaire. They are jumbled here because they are grouped by the intelligence that they indicate. The intelligences will be discussed over the following pages. You are likely to have some ticks in most areas, but a higher number of ticks in two or three. However, there is no wrong answer - everyone is different. You may find that you prefer to learn in one way, or a large variety of ways…

Interpersonal

People tend to fall into one or other of the personal categories, which stand slightly apart from the other five categories. It is likely that you scored higher in one of these two categories than the other and unlikely you scored nothing in either category.

If you want to develop your interpersonal intelligence, try the following:

▶ Ring your mum after lectures and explain all the concepts you have learned in the day

▶ Pick three items of news out of the newspaper every day and discuss them with someone else.

▶ Join a debating club

▶ Volunteer to help out at a children's club or school

Interpersonal people are those people who find it natural to *interact heavily with other people* in the thought and learning process.

They will regularly *question* a person who is teaching them, they will *discuss* what they have learned with other people, they will seek to understand things through *conversing* through them, they would be happy to *summarise* what they have learned *for other people*.

These people are likely to be natural teachers or salespeople, *communicating with others comes naturally* to them. They may find they do the following:

▶ Interact with groups of other people without concern

▶ Bounce ideas off other people

▶ Talk things through with people if they are worried about something

▶ Brainstorm corporately (with others)

Interpersonal people

" Liz is a **people person.** "

" Frank always knows the right thing to say. I always go to him if I'm down or want advice. "

12

Intrapersonal

Intrapersonal people are people who *think things through themselves* before discussing them with others. They are likely to be *self-aware* and good managers of themselves.

They may find that communicating with others does not come naturally to them. This does not mean that they are not good at it when they do communicate with others.

An intrapersonal person might do the following:

- Keep their thoughts to themselves
- Reflect on issues before coming to a conclusion
- Often seek time alone to think
- Brainstorm privately

To develop your skills, you could try the following:

- *Pick three topics out of the newspaper every day, and consciously spend ten minutes thinking through the issues you see being raised.*

- *When you want to ask a question, stop. Note the question down, but allow yourself some time to think through the question raised and see if you can come up with the answer yourself.*

These 'personal' intelligences will have strong links with your other key intelligences, which you will see as you read through the following pages.

For example, a linguistic interpersonal person may communicate in words, a spatial visual intrapersonal person may think things through in pictures.

Intrapersonal people

"Amir is a reflective person - **he always gives a well thought out answer.**"

"Susan is a think-tank. She'll sort through an idea for you."

Linguistic

> **I find ...**
>
> When I have worked through illustrations such as the questionnaire you completed earlier in this Chapter, I have found that I come out as highly linguistic.
>
> This makes sense to me. I love words, enjoy observing correlation and links between different languages, am a writer, enjoy games such as 'Articulate'.

This may also be true for you. If it is not, however, you may want to try and develop your linguistic intelligence by trying some of the following things:

- *Reading magazines/books on subjects which interest you*
- *Challenging yourself to learn ten new words a week*
- *Telling your mirror two minutes worth of interesting information every morning.*

Linguistic people are those people who are comfortable with and enjoy language, or words.

Not every linguistic person will enjoy all the same things, but the following is a list of things which a linguistic person might find interesting, enjoy or relate to more easily than another type of person would.

- ▶ Word games
- ▶ Reading
- ▶ Making speeches
- ▶ Poetry
- ▶ Learning other languages
- ▶ Grammar
- ▶ Crosswords
- ▶ Thesauruses

Being linguistic does not mean you will be very good at writing - you may never have learned to write - but that you enjoy words. This can reveal itself in the fact that you love to talk, or read, that is, any activity that involves words as opposed to pictures.

Ant   Bag   Crystallisation

Linguistic people

" Betty's really got the **gift of the gab.** "

" Jason's a total bookworm. He's always got his head stuck in a book. "

14

Mathematical logical

Mathematical logical people are people who are comfortable with and enjoy numbers, and a system of thought which follows a certain reason. Such people are often analysts, and very rational.

Accountants are commonly drawn from mathematical logical stock, so don't be surprised if you fall into this category. However, also don't be alarmed if you do not: accountants call on a great variety of skills, that is part of the challenge of studying to become an accountant.

Here is a list of activities or thoughts that a mathematical logical person may enjoy or relate to:

- ▶ Number puzzles
- ▶ Rubic cube
- ▶ Logic puzzles
- ▶ 'Cluedo'
- ▶ Prioritisation
- ▶ Patterns

Mathematical logical people can come into their own if you are on a budget in the supermarket and you've forgotten your calculator, because they are usually quick with numbers and can do mental arithmetic.

They are also useful if you want to remember a phone number or a date.

> *Mathematical logical people are the people who when they watch thrillers or detective films can work out 'whodunnit' before the ending is revealed. If you are not one, you must know one…always one step ahead of Poirot, analysing, considering, never suspending their disbelief…*
>
> *If you want to develop your mathematical logical intelligence, try one or more of the following activities:*
>
> - ▶ *Become a scorer for a darts or cricket team*
> - ▶ *Challenge yourself to grocery shop to a budget without a calculator*
> - ▶ *Get someone to quiz you in mental arithmetic over breakfast.*

Mathematical logical people

"Pawandeep has always had a head for figures."

"Rick's as sharp as a knife. One day he'll cut himself"

Spatial visual

The spatial side of spatial visual is a little bit difficult to explain or possibly to understand.

*It is people who seem to be at **one with their environment**, **seem never** to **get lost** - so are good natural **navigators**. They **notice things around them**, so that they can identify where they are in relation to their surroundings.*

They can also judge space by sight, so for example, as stated below, they would be able to judge easily whether their car would fit into a parking space by looking at it.

If you want to develop your spatial visual intelligence, try some of the following:

- ▶ *Go somewhere you don't know as a passenger (by car or bus) and focus on noticing your environment. Then try to navigate back again.*

- ▶ *Try some simple drawing or diagramming.*

Spatial visual people are those people who are comfortable with or enjoy their spatial environment (the things that are around them) and visual things such as pictures and art.

Again, this does not mean that they are necessarily great artists. It means that they prefer pictures to words. It means that if someone is telling them about something, they can picture the scene, or if they do read books, they can strongly visualise the characters and scenes as they unfold.

As always, not everyone who displays spatial visual tendencies will enjoy the same things, but the following is a list of activities and concepts that a spatial visual person might enjoy or relate to:

- ▶ Drawing
- ▶ Cartoons
- ▶ Films
- ▶ Treasure hunts
- ▶ Orienteering
- ▶ Mindmaps

Spatial visual people

" Katie's got an amazing **sense of direction.** "

" Phil always parks the car - he can always tell whether the car will fit in the space. "

Musical

Musical people are those people who are comfortable with, and enjoy, music, rhyme and/or rhythm.

Again, a person who falls into the musical category may not find that they like or are comfortable with all these things, but rather one or two, or a selection. There may be a strong overlap between a linguistic person who enjoys poetry for the words and also the musical side of poetry in the metre and rhyme. Alternatively, a musical person might not appreciate rhyme, but have perfect pitch or be able to play any musical instrument available.

Here is a list of activities that a musical person may enjoy:

- Attending concerts
- Listening to a walkman or radio
- Creating limericks
- Playing a musical instrument
- Humming/whistling/singing in the shower
- Dancing

Musical intelligence may not be something we recognise in ourselves if we have never played an instrument, or had any formal musical training.

Remember that in this analysis, you are trying to *get back to the basics of how you think, not how you have been trained in life to date*.

You may not play any musical instruments, but if you *hear music* in your head on a regular basis, or *get an urge to drum anything* in front of you that has a vaguely flat surface, then you probably fall into this category.

If you want to develop your musical intelligence, why not try the following:

- Fill five pint glasses with varying levels of water and *create a sonata* by tapping them with a spoon.
- Pick two words a day and try to think of ten words that *rhyme* with them (you could then write a nonsense poem if it took your fancy).

Musical people

"Ella's just got **rhythm, man**"

"John's always humming or whistling - always got a tune."

17

Bodily kinaesthetic

Bodily kinaesthetic people are those people who often seem to have 'magic hands'. They make the rest of us seem very clumsy, as they are **well co-ordinated** and in control of their bodies.

They tend to be termed practical because they can 'do' things. It is often observed of good footballers that 'they can **do things** with that football that I can only dream of...', for example, free kicks which seem only to have been tickled and yet which burst a hole in the top corner of the net.

If you want to develop your bodily kinaesthetic intelligence, you might try:

▶ Taking up a racquet sport

▶ Playing the game where you have to negotiate a piece of wire around a wire frame without touching the frame and causing the game to buzz.

Bodily kinaesthetic people are people who are comfortable with, and enjoy, doing things and being active. They are most likely to learn how to do something if they are shown how to do it, and then do it for themselves.

This is likely to mean that they are 'trial and error' people, that is, people who don't mind making mistakes the first time, because if they keep doing something they will get it right in the end. They understood the theory they were told in school that 'practice makes perfect'.

Here is a list of activities or thoughts that a bodily kinaesthetic person may enjoy or relate to:

▶ Sport
▶ Craft
▶ Design and technology
▶ 'Hands on' experience
▶ Good hand-eye co-ordination
▶ Games like 'Jenga' and 'Pick up stix'

Bodily kinaesthetic people

❝Peter is really good with **his hands.**❞

❝Mai's got amazing hand-eye co-ordination.❞

18

Analysing the elephant

In the light of what you have read over the previous 7 pages about the different types of intelligence that we possess, look back at what you produced in illustration 2.

Does what you produced reflect the results of your questionnaire?

For example, a person who strongly portrays linguistic intelligence will have used words to describe an elephant, a visual person may have doodled bits of elephant, for example, tusks, big ears, trunk.

A maths-logical person may have approached the issue by recognising groups of ideas, for example by using headings such as habitat, appearance etc…

A musical person may have written a rhyme, or thought immediately of the song 'Nellie the Elephant'.

A bodily kinaesthetic person may have written nothing or lots down, but not before they instinctively raised their arm to their face like a trunk (or wanted to!).

Elephants

Elephants are mammals found particularly in Africa and the Indian subcontinent.

They are characterised by their large trunks and their distinctive tusks which have long been the target of poachers…

The elephant is seen as being a very wise animal, hence the saying that 'an elephant never forgets…'

Ivory → Poachers

Tusks   Africa   Memory

ELEPHANTS

Mammal

Habitat	Features	Other aspects
Africa	Tusk	Ivory
Indian sub-continent	Trunk	Poaching
Trees	Big ears	Memory
Plains	Molars	

An elephant is big and grey
And in the mud he likes to play
He never will forget a thing
And his great trunk he likes to swing
He pushes down trees to eat their bark
Hence he leaves his special mark
I like the African best I fear,
Because I like his great big ears

Nellie the elephant packed her trunk, and said goodbye to the circus …

The results of the elephant illustration

This is not a sure-fire illustration, because we have all been taught to respond in a certain way, and it is possible that although the illustration did not tell you to write, **you made an assumption** that you were **to use words**, because that is how you usually answer questions.

However, think back to your initial responses to the instruction and see if they fit with the intelligence brackets which you have identified yourself with.

Further analysis

Here is a series of questions for you to think about. This time, instead of just giving your gut answer, think about why you have given that answer and what it shows about the type of intelligence you prefer to use.

Some pointers are given to help you think these through.

Q Are you the sort of person who will observe, 'I hate to watch a film when I've read the book'?

Did you answer

Yes?
... because I hate to watch videos — Does this indicate you are not very **visual?**
...because the film spoils the pictures in my head — Are you **visual?**

No?
...because I never read books — Does this indicate you are not **linguistic?**
...because I am indifferent to this sentence — Are you neither **visual** or **linguistic?**

Q If I was to tell you that the next thing that I am going to tell you will be true, but the last thing I told you was a lie, would you believe me?

Did you answer

Yes? ... because I see no reason to disbelieve you — Does this indicate you have not noticed the flawed **logic** in this sentence?

No? ...because the sentence cannot be true — Still not quite getting the **logic...**

Nothing? ...because you know the sentence is not logical — Are you **logical?**

Did you think it through or go away and talk it through with a group of friends? (Are you intrapersonal or interpersonal?)

Think about it!

Next time someone else (or even you) says something along these lines, spend a moment wondering why they are saying it. Perhaps you might even ask them what their reasoning was. It is probably because they are showing an **intellectual preference**. Only some of the intelligences have been illustrated here. There are endless examples:

A **musical** person might be annoyed by inaccurate tuning on a radio that you have not even noticed...
A **bodily kinaesthetic** person may be irritated by an activity that requires them to sit still...
Someone who is **intrapersonal** might find a fast-paced lecture with no breaks difficult - they haven't had a chance to think...

Visual, aural or practical?

Before we leave this chapter, it doesn't hurt to explore your preferences between visual, aural or practical learning. There are some obvious links between these concepts and the intelligences we have just outlined (these are indicated in the right hand column) but the links do not have to, and may not, be obvious in your case.

Try the following questions, noting your preferences in terms of most preferred (1) to least preferred (3), with (2) being the one in the middle.

A When I am learning something, I would rather:

Hear it	☐	**A**
Read it	☐	**V**
Do it myself	☐	**P**

B In leisure time I like to:

Go to the cinema	☐	**V**
Do something active	☐	**P**
Go to a concert	☐	**A**

C I would be annoyed by:

Colour clashes	☐	**V**
Dissonance	☐	**A**
Physical restraint	☐	**P**

D I am indifferent to:

Work experience	☐	**P**
Lectures	☐	**A**
Libraries	☐	**V**

VISUAL LEARNING
⬇
SPATIAL VISUAL PEOPLE

Consider also that linguistic people may prefer to read words than to hear them ...

AURAL LEARNING
⬇
MUSICAL PEOPLE

PRACTICAL LEARNING
⬇
BODILY KINAESTHETIC PEOPLE

> *The **implications** of these questions **may seem obvious**, but it is a **useful exercise** just to prompt us about how we prefer to receive teaching, which we might not have been able to identify so easily.*

E I am irritated by:

Changes in light quality	☐	**V**
Changes in temperature	☐	**P**
Persistent, unintentional noises	☐	**A**

F When trying to concentrate I would notice:

Sirens	☐	**A**
Flashing lights	☐	**V**
Whether I am still or not	☐	**P**

G If I was teaching someone else something, I would:

Show them	☐	**P**
Tell them	☐	**A**
Make them a note of it	☐	**V**

Analysing this questionnaire

Look back over the last two pages and tot up your total scores for 'P', 'V' and 'A' statements. If you have one which is lower than the others, you are likely to have a clear preference for how you receive information, if you have similar scores for each, you appear to be indifferent between methods of receiving information.

Lastly, cast your mind back over the ways you have been given information in the past and what your experiences of that have been, just to check this indication is correct. If this suggests you are highly aural, yet you hated lectures at University, have you been totally honest in your answers? Of course, you may just have been subjected to some poor lectures ...

And finally ...

One last observation about learning styles

Broadly speaking, people carry two attitudes into studying.

These are summarised to the right.

Which do you feel you most identify with?

Neither of the positions is right or wrong. However, as with all the things we have discussed so far, it is best to identify what your prevailing attitude is, so that you can incorporate that understanding into your approach to your study and study materials.

Why?

If you are the kind of person that feels that they will not be able to come to terms with a theory unless they have been given a chance to '**see it in action**' or at least understand where the theory will be **relevant in practice**, you may find the idea of opening a text book and wading through theory very off-putting.

There is a solution which you might consider. When approaching study materials, flick through looking for case examples or questions. Reading through these should **indicate the practicalities of a theory** before you get into the 'nitty gritty'.

What?

If you prefer to **get to grips with a theory** before you start implanting it in practical situations, do the opposite. **Read through the theory once or twice before reading any case examples or questions**. When you feel that you have nailed the theory - then look to see how it applies in practice and in the exam.

---

*Some people like to think practically. They are prepared to learn theory, but only after they can clearly see why it is needed in practice, and how the theory will be put to use. This is what we are going to refer to as the '**WHY?**' position.*

*Some people like theory. They prefer to get to grips with what the theory is before they start thinking about how to put it into practice. This is what we are going to refer to as the '**WHAT?**' position.*

Learning styles actions points

Now that you have identified your intelligences and your preferences for receiving information, you should do several things:

- ▶ Note your preferences
- ▶ Read through the rest of this book to see how you can **apply** your preferences to your studies
- ▶ Note which of your intelligences you are not using
- ▶ Consider whether you should try and develop any of them (using the exercises given previously)

Types of subject

Introduction

Having looked at *how* you learn in the last chapter, in this chapter we're going to move onto *what* you will be learning.

Accountancy exams are designed to equip you with the **knowledge** and **skills** necessary to perform well at increasing levels of responsibility.

Framework of exams

Exams are organised within a framework that reflects different levels of responsibility. There are variations in the framework used by different accounting bodies; the example below is the most common and it illustrates the progression of skills that all bodies aim to achieve.

1 Foundation level papers examine the core skills (such as use of procedures, methods and communication) that everyone working as an accountant should have

2 Intermediate level papers test more advanced technical topics that someone in a senior role would have to know, and also involve more complicated situations

3 Final or professional level papers are primarily concerned with managerial skills such as problem solving and developing strategy

The subjects you'll be studying

The second half of the chapter is devoted to the most important subject areas for exams. We won't be using a lot of jargon in these pages, but we shall show you the main things you have to do to pass.

This chapter will demonstrate what you need to achieve in your studies.

We shall look at each level in more detail over the next few pages.

What we'd like you to do when you read the remaining chapters of this book is remind yourself constantly what you need to demonstrate to the examiner. Ask yourself how different study skills and revision techniques can help you pass.

Are you worried about coping with subjects that involve lots of numbers?

or

Are you concerned about having to write lots of essays for certain subjects?

If you answered yes to either question, turn to page 31.

Foundation exams

> *The entries in the accounting records have to be organised and summarised if they are to be useful to the accountant.*

The hows

The basic skill that you'll learn at Foundation level is how to make entries in accounting records. You will also learn how to use information contained in those records.

- Classifying information into different categories
- Aggregating and summarising information by preparing accounts

And the whys

Foundation exams will also give you an introduction into the theory of accountancy. This involves becoming familiar with accounting terminology. You will also need to have some knowledge of wider accounting concepts that influence how you treat and interpret information.

Similarly learning techniques at this level is not just about learning a series of mechanical processes. Even at this stage, you need to develop a critical understanding of what you are doing.

- When you should use the techniques
- The limitations of the techniques

> *This will be a fundamental point throughout your studies; learning a technique means learning how to use it intelligently, not unthinkingly.*

Examination methods

Most Foundation level papers these days will test you by means of multiple choice or short answer questions. (Indeed, in many cases you may be required to answer these questions on a computer.) Papers that require longer answers will examine your communication skills, your ability to present information logically and clearly in various formats.

You may be asked to
- State (express or detail clearly)
- Describe (communicate key features)

Exemptions

If you are taking certain qualifications, you may be exempt from some or all of the lowest level papers. However when you study higher level papers, you will be expected to know topics that were covered at Foundation level. You may therefore have to spend time studying these areas before moving onto more advanced topics, in particular in the core subjects of financial accounting and management accounting.

Intermediate exams

More ability

You will be expected to have more expertise than at Foundation level. Therefore you have to learn about more complex topics and more advanced techniques, applied to more complicated situations.

More analysis

You will also find out more about how data is used in the planning, control and decision-making processes. You will use a range of measures, financial and non-financial, to judge performance.

More authority

The papers will test how skilful you are in various aspects of a supervisory role.

- ▶ Exercising control
- ▶ Designing, managing and evaluating systems
- ▶ Interpreting results, identifying problems and deciding how they will be investigated

The way forward

You will also start to find out about the wider strategic decisions businesses make, which you will study further at final level, in particular certain critical choices.

- ▶ Sources of finance
- ▶ Investment decisions

At Foundation level the techniques you have to use will normally be clearly signposted. The situations you encounter at Intermediate level will not be so clear cut (more like real-life in fact).

Exams will test how good you are at supervising day-to-day operations, and how you can contribute effectively to project development.

Key techniques

Making a big effort to grasp techniques will not only secure you a pass at Intermediate level, but will also benefit you at Final level, where many techniques learned at Intermediate level will be needed again.

Final exams

Examples of key decisions

- ▶ Merging/taking over other companies
- ▶ Managing business risks

Key skills

- ▶ Linking different techniques
- ▶ Bringing in material from other subjects
- ▶ Using knowledge of the local and international business environments
- ▶ Discussing developments and controversies

The ultimate test

Most final level exams will test how you would cope in a senior management role, taking key business decisions. In some subjects you will not be an employee of the organisation described in the question; you will however be in a equivalent senior role, a business adviser or audit partner for example.

The wide strategic perspective

You will have to show that you can recommend and justify strategic decisions, concerned with the overall long-term direction of organisations. These decisions will demand awareness of the internal and external situation, also the implications of organisations' mission and goals. You will need to think widely about the problems organisations face and demonstrate commercial awareness.

How you're examined

Often in final level papers you will be given a business situation that reflects, or is drawn from, real-life examples. You will have to use selectively the knowledge, theory and techniques you have learned at lower levels to analyse the information you are given and make recommendations.

> You will be writing reports that will be read by recipients specified in the question; what you write must be tailored to your readership's needs and demands.

Remember

that you will primarily be tested on your ability to provide realistic business advice, with less emphasis on technical knowledge than at earlier stages.

Words and numbers

You may have one of two views on how your studies will go.

1 You feel that the written papers should not be too demanding, but you will struggle with papers involving lots of calculations, as you've never been very good at maths.

2 You don't think you'll have any problems with the numbers, but you've always found writing long essays more challenging.

If you're unhappy with the calculations ...

Most of the techniques you will use in accountancy papers are not mathematically difficult; it's more a case of knowing the steps to follow. The final answer to long calculations needn't be correct for you to pass; what you must remember is that you can gain sufficient marks by getting certain stages right.

If you're unhappy with the essays ...

Examiners rarely complain that students cannot express themselves in words. More common sources of complaint are answers being untidy and lacking a clear layout, and answers containing irrelevant material.

If you can do calculations efficiently, you will give yourself more time to set out your written answers well.

Key steps are:
- *Do the easy calculations*
- *Set out your workings clearly*
- *Discuss the results of your calculations and their limitations*

You needn't be a wordy (linguistic) person to set your work out well and answer the question being asked.

Remember

that you will see **lots** of questions that require you to carry out calculations **and** provide commentary.

The subjects you'll study

Active review

In chapter 4 we shall talk about how you should review the material you have learned so that you can recall it better. Review can just mean reading through your notes again. However answering a question or doing an exercise is normally a much better test of how well you have understood what you have studied.

That's an introduction to an exercise we'd like you to do. We've listed below eight main subject areas that are tested in the exams of most or all accountancy bodies.

- Financial accounts (for shareholders/external users)
- Auditing (checking the truth and fairness of accounts)
- Management accounts (for internal managers)
- Financial management
- Information technology
- Management
- Tax
- Law

For each subject area

- State the learning styles covered in chapter 1 that you think will be of greatest assistance when studying the subject

In the remainder of this chapter, we shall give you some answers for this exercise, and also provide you with an indication of the main themes that run through each subject.

Bear in mind that you'll study certain subjects at more than one level. You'll also need to think about why you encounter subjects at some levels but not others.

Top tips

We shall also include a tip that will help you study more effectively. Bear in mind that most of the tips apply to more than one subject. For example finding out common mistakes students keep making (the tax tip) will benefit you in other subjects as well.

Financial accounting

Financial accounts are monetary statements summarising an organisation's performance during a period and its position at the period-end. You will have to prepare accounts in a variety of formats according to rules laid down in law and accounting standards.

> Examples of typical financial accounting questions are 'Prepare a set of group accounts' or 'Prepare a cash flow statement in accordance with Financial Reporting Standard 1.'

This is likely to be good news for bodily-kinaesthetic people.

However you will also need to understand the logic behind the accounting rules so that you can explain the treatment of items within accounts. For higher level papers, you may have to criticise current or proposed regulations.

> An example would be 'Discuss the current problems relating to the treatment of leases in financial statements.'

Intrapersonal people should find this aspect interesting.

You will also have to examine accounts and interpret the messages they give, highlighting the aspects of most interest to readers.

> You might be asked to prepare a report for the chairman of a group of companies, comparing the business and financial performance of two companies within the group.

People with musical abilities should enjoy trying to identify patterns within a set of data.

Top tip

Remember that financial accounting papers can be wide-ranging; even if you do find the preparation of certain types of accounts difficult, don't spend **all** your time practising them. You need to ensure that you can answer other questions that do not involve the preparation of accounts.

Auditing

Auditors look to gather evidence by reviewing a business's accounts and records so that they can give an opinion. External auditors, who are not employees of the company, give opinions on the reliability of accounts.

Often in questions your role will be the senior member of the external audit team on site, responsible for the detailed work being completed. You will therefore have to decide how best to gain evidence about the organisation's systems, transactions, assets and liabilities.

> A typical question would give you details that relate to an audit area, and ask what you need to find out about that area and the audit procedures you would use.

Questions also reflect the need for you to follow up problems if you find them, and to act professionally and ethically in sensitive situations.

> You might be asked what you need to investigate in a particular situation, or to describe what you should do when your firm is threatened with removal from office as an auditor.

For higher level papers, you will be asked about more complicated audits, also assignments other than audits. You will also have to show that you can take the kind of management decisions that audit partners (in overall charge of the external audit) would take.

> These include decisions about whether to accept appointment as an auditor and on overall audit strategy for a particular client.

Hence you need to be able to decide which audit tests are relevant for the client's circumstances, and if necessary, devise some of your own; this may appeal if you are a bodily kinaesthetic person.

Dealing with clients effectively doesn't just mean quoting the auditing rulebook every time there's a problem; it also involves the use of interpersonal skills.

Top tip

Give sufficient detail of what is being audited. For example don't just say:

"Check expenditure is correctly stated"

SAY

"Check expenditure is correctly stated by comparing payments in the cash book with purchase invoices and other supporting documentation"

Management accounting

Understanding why different types of data (above all cost data) are important is fundamental in management accounting. You will learn about various ways of classifying, analysing and using data.

Although a lot of these techniques can be learned as a step approach, you will also need to understand why different methods are used, and in what circumstances; remember at higher levels you will have to select for yourself the best techniques.

Bodily-kinaesthetic people might enjoy applying these techniques.

For intermediate level papers, you will study techniques that are used for the purpose of controlling the organisation. These include planning, resource allocation and investigation of variations from what was expected. As you are promoted, you will become accountable for how your department performs; you therefore need to understand the significance and limitations of various performance measures.

A lot of questions will involve setting budgets, or considering how actual performance differed from the standards that should have been achieved.

An important aspect of management accounting measures is how they affect people's behaviour, so interpersonal skills will be useful here.

Your management accounting skills will ultimately be used to assess the effects of strategic decisions, including decisions about pricing, product ranges and marketing.

You may be asked to discuss the decisions and the methods that can be used to measure whether the goals set have been achieved.

We mentioned earlier that accountancy is like a language. Management accountants have to explain the meaning of the data they use to non-financial decision-makers. They may also have to make assumptions on the basis of imperfect information and to be aware of the limitations of the data.

Top tip

Remember always to do every part of each question! A common theme in examiners' reports in management accounting papers is candidates spending all their time on calculations, and neglecting question parts involving written discussion.

Financial management

Finance is a vital element in business planning and decision-making, and financial management therefore covers many of the key decisions businesses make. At the heart of this subject are the sources of finance businesses have available, the management of these sources and how the finance available affects business decisions.

> Questions range from considering the appropriateness of various finance sources to assessing the consequences of choosing different mixes of finance.

At intermediate level you will study day-to-day management of cash and other current assets and liabilities.

> The main current assets and liabilities are goods held in stock, balances owing from customers, and balances owed to suppliers.

You will also learn how to value companies and to appraise investments. These techniques are then used to support decision-making at higher levels, when you will examine the impact of major investment decisions upon business strategy.

> A very common subject of questions is whether one company should buy another company.

Another important topic is how businesses manage financial risks that could seriously threaten their existence. These include the risk of important sources of finance no longer being available, also the risks businesses face from currency or interest rate movements.

> **Thus financial management is not a mechanical subject, but involves the intrapersonal skill of thinking through the implications of major decisions.**

> **Maths logical people may enjoy calculating the impact of different risk management policies.**

Top tip

Financial management is not just a textbook subject; regular reading of the business pages of newspapers will provide real-life examples of the decisions and factors you will be discussing when considering financial strategy.

There is rarely a right or wrong answer in management questions especially at higher level.

Information technology

Information technology papers are not primarily about details of the latest technological developments.

> Although you do need to know about commonly used hardware and software, you must also appreciate what qualities information needs to possess (this is also essential for the accounting papers).

Information systems are very important, reflecting the fact that you must be aware of the information you need to do your job. As well as the design and development of information systems, you will also be tested on their implementation, control and evaluation.

> A typical question would cover the various stages of a systems project.

Exams for higher level papers focus on the part information systems play in the strategic management of the organisation. You will learn how information technology is changing the nature and structure of the working environment, and how use of information systems can give businesses competitive advantages.

> You will often be given a business situation that has several aspects which you need to discuss. You would not only consider the links between information and business strategy, but wider managerial and environmental issues as well.

Spatial-visual people should cope well with questions that cover construction of systems, and what systems are needed for particular environments.

Mathematical-logical people may be able to spot system flaws!

Top tip

Do not spend too much time mastering the technical intricacies of computer systems, however interesting you find them. The exams are not designed to turn you into an information technology specialist. Examiners often complain that higher level answers contain too much technical detail, and not enough discussion on how information technology can be used to fulfil a business's objectives.

Management

Management papers test your ability to take decisions and solve problems. The management theory and the analysis methods that you study will help you develop solutions.

> Ultimately you will be studying strategic management, the development, implementation and control of strategies.

Management papers at intermediate level tend to concentrate on matters affecting business operations. These include human resources, relationships within an organisation and management culture. Management of change is also very important.

> Examples of problems that you might encounter include introducing effective recruitment policies, or taking steps to overcome resistance to change.

Both intrapersonal (thinking a problem through to its solution) and interpersonal (where you appreciate the human dimension) skills are important here.

At the highest levels you will be required to evaluate strategic options, bearing in mind the consequences of, and constraints upon, the various options.

> Most higher level papers include compulsory longer questions, worth 50% or more of the marks. You will be given a lot of detail about an organisation and have to provide recommendations for future strategy.

The spatial visual skill of being able to visualise the environments within which strategies will be developed will be useful.

Management papers will also test skills and knowledge you have learned in other papers. These include use of financial information and performance measurement criteria to evaluate strategy, and the impact of technological developments.

Top tip

Remember that no management model is applicable in all circumstances. You will have to select the most appropriate model and apply it to the question where relevant.

There is rarely a right or wrong answer in management questions, especially at higher level.

Tax

Tax is an important topic in accountancy exams, as most people in general accounting roles will deal with some tax issues; tax is not always left to specialists. All managers need an appreciation of the tax impacts of decisions they are taking.

Most accountancy bodies first examine tax at intermediate level. You will need to know the detailed technical rules, and be able to apply them in calculating tax and possibly reporting your findings. The most important technique in tax papers is the tax computation.

> Calculating the tax individuals or companies owe on their income is at the heart of tax papers.

Higher level papers will require you to act as a tax adviser. This will involve understanding your clients' objectives at various stages of their lives, and recommending strategies that will result in tax charges being avoided or deferred. The onus will be on you to recognise which taxes are relevant.

> You may therefore be asked to assess the suitability of different courses of action, bearing in mind the tax consequences of each and the personal or business circumstances of your client.

Tax will often appeal to maths logical people who enjoy carrying out long calculations, following a set of prescribed rules.

Top tip

Examiners' reports offer a good guide to aspects of tax that candidates get wrong sitting after sitting after sitting. Knowing what these are and making sure you get them right can **significantly** enhance your chances of passing.

Law

Accountants need to be able to recognise issues of legal significance when they encounter them in their day-to-day work, even though they are not being trained as lawyers. Hence law has always formed part of accountancy syllabuses.

Law is now often tested at Foundation level, the main aim being to test knowledge, in particular breadth of knowledge.

> Hence law at this level is often tested by means of multiple-choice or other short answer questions. The more questions there are, the greater the number of areas of law that can be tested, and the greater the assurance gained that students who pass the exam have sufficiently wide-ranging knowledge.

Linguistic people may enjoy studying the detail that you need to know to do well in law.

Where law is examined at intermediate level, some questions will ask you to outline features of the legal system or state a body of law.

> For example you may be asked to explain the importance of the courts in the legal system, or what details company documents should contain.

You may however be given questions which require the skills of being able to recognise legal problems, apply the law to the situation described and communicate your analysis to interested parties.

Scenario questions will call upon intrapersonal skills, the ability to think issues through to a conclusion.

> These will involve fictional scenarios with details that are similar to one or a number of decided cases, where a number of legal points arise.

Top tip

For law papers where questions come in a variety of formats, you need to find out how different areas are most likely to be tested. Specific rules will often be tested by multiple-choice questions, areas where the main law is statute-based by 'state the law' type questions, and areas where there is a lot of case law by fictional scenarios.

- Learning styles
- Types of subject
- Study environment
- Study skills
- Revision
- Types of question
- Exam paper

Study environment

Study environment

```
                    Relaxation                              Lounge
        Commitment                          Bedroom                    ?
                Motivation                          Home
        Focus                                               Library
              ( Mental     )                College              Office
              ( preparation)                      ( Place )
                    ↖                              ↗
                       Why?              Where?
                            ( STUDY      )
                            (ENVIRONMENT )
                       When?             How?
                    ↙                              ↘
                ( Time )                    ( Ambience )
                                                    Noise
        When?           How long for?
                                       Company              Decor
             How frequently?
                                  Fellow students  Friends
```

Introduction

The mind map above outlines the factors that make up this Chapter. Having previously looked at how you prefer to receive and process information, and having taken a look at the nature of the subjects you are likely to have to study, we shall now explore the environment in which you study.

Mental preparation

In the next few pages we are going to address four aspects of being mentally prepared for your accountancy studies. Perhaps the most important is motivation. When setting yourself out to do something you are aware will be challenging, it is important to be clear in your own mind why you are doing it.

We will also touch on commitment. The nature and timetable of any accountancy exams mean that you have made a big commitment to your training. This is closely linked with motivation. You have made the commitment because you want to achieve the goal: qualification.

It is wrong to concentrate too much on the difficulties of training. We don't want to put you off! It is also important to relax into studying, as your brain works better when it is relaxed, so we will look a little at the question of relaxation.

Lastly, we shall look at focus, which is strongly linked with the other aspects of mental preparation discussed.

Motivation

Commitment

Relaxation

Focus

Why?

*Training to be an accountant is a **tough task** - don't let anyone tell you differently.*

*Anyone who has trained as an accountant would tell you they had days when the **WHY of training** to be an accountant loomed large and they were not sure how to answer it.*

*If you have started out on this course then there is no doubt that you have made a **substantial commitment** to your career, and to a certain way of life for a period of time.*

*It is therefore very important that you **prepare yourself mentally** for the prospect of both training and studying to be an accountant.*

This book deals in the main with the studying side, in practice you will find that the two overlap.

Were you ever a boy scout or girl guide? When facing training as an accountant, it is a good idea to borrow the scouts' motto:

Be prepared

Motivation

Take a moment to think, and then jot down the reason (s) why you are studying to be an accountant, in the space given below.

Was this a cinch for you? Do you have a clear idea of why you have got yourself into this, or was it quite hard for you to identify why you are doing it?

Whatever the reason you have written down in the box to the left is, it is unlikely that you have written nothing. Getting a place on a course to study accountancy, or a training contract with a firm of accountants is not an easy thing to do, so you must have put some effort into it. That type of effort rarely comes without a reason.

Sometimes people go into things because they couldn't think of anything better to do. That is **not a good reason**. That will **not motivate you** through at least three years of hard work in your (sometimes minimal) spare time and a string of challenging exams. You had better re-think your reason quickly.

Studying is easier if your brain wants to learn. It is very important to be motivated to learn. Motivation is a key learning tool. It will help to improve your concentration, and it will drive your commitment to your studies. A key part of preparing to learn is identifying your motivation. You have just done that in the box to the left.

Training to be an accountant takes a long time. It can be easy to forget this motivation. Your motivation may change or waver over the coming months and years. You may think our next suggestion is the most stupid thing that you have ever heard, or you may think that it will be helpful. It's up to you:

Write out your motivation on a sheet of paper and tack it above your desk, carve it into your pencil case and put it in your diary.

KEEP IT with you.
You will **NEED IT.**

Motivation

"I want to qualify and have my own independent practice."

"I want to command a good salary with great prospects"

"I've always wanted to be an accountant - now I've got all the right grades so far and a place with a training firm, so I'm really going to go for it!"

Commitment

Time commitment

We will discuss time management and timetables later in this Chapter. One thing is clear. In order to successfully complete accountancy training, you *must be prepared to commit time to learning*.

Time sacrifice

Whether you are studying accountancy or not, there are *still the same number of hours in a day*. It is possible that in making your commitment to accountancy, you may have to *divert time* to accountancy from other activities.

In other words you may have to make a time sacrifice. You may want to mentally or through writing in the space given to the left, sacrifice some activities to commit time to accountancy.

Commitment

Commitment **stems from motivation** and has a strong link with **time management,** which we will look at later in this Chapter.

MOTIVATION ➔ **COMMITMENT**
I want this Therefore I will put time into it ...

Relaxation

> **Some relaxation exercises for you to try:**
>
> *Exercise one*
>
> Lie on the floor and tense up all your muscles. Then, working from your toes upwards, relax each one in turn until you are completely relaxed.
>
> *Exercise two*
>
> Run a bath will warm water and relaxing aromatherapy oils. Play your favourite piece of relaxing music. Get in the bath…
>
> *Exercise three*
>
> Make sure you are the only person in the house. Choose some rock or dance music and play it loudly. Headbang or dance away your frustrations until you can relax and study.

TENSE BRAIN = NOT COOPERATIVE

It is scientifically agreed that a relaxed brain is more receptive to learning than a tense one. Trust me, it is something to do with neurones, electricity, brain waves, synapses or something … Let's leave the science to the scientists and just enjoy the fact that from now on, despite the fact that we are studying, we have to make sure that we are relaxed.

Several things have an impact on relaxation:

1 Time (see page 55) Schedule **time off.** Schedule study time **sensibly.**

2 Ambience (see page 52) **Know** what helps you to relax **before** you sit down to study.

3 Support The support **BPP** offers is discussed below.

You will also require the support of your friends and family. You may have to ask them to help out with things such as creating a good study atmosphere, giving you time to study and so on…

Support from BPP

If you are booked on a BPP Home Study or Classroom course and you are tense about your study, do not suffer in silence. BPP offers on-line and telephone support for when you do not understand an element of your studies. **Call, discuss, relax…**

Focus

Concentration checklist

Movement
When you sit down to study are you in place that you can be still in? Or are you going to be disturbed (for example, if you work on the kitchen table, or the bus…)? Movement is likely to break up your concentration.

Vision
When you sit down to study are you in a place with nothing very interesting to look at? Or are things going to catch your attention (for example if you sit by a window, or opposite the front door)? Your eyes will be drawn - end of concentration. See page 53

Temperature
When you sit down to study are you in a place that is unusually hot or cold, or where the temperature will fluctuate? You will have personal preferences about temperature, but changes in it may adversely affect your concentration. See page 53

Noise
When you sit down to study, do you have control over the noises you hear, or is the place noisy? (Examples, you control the music in your own room, but not the traffic on the street.) Uninvited noise may affect your concentration. See page 53

Intentions
When you sit down to study do you have a clear work plan in your head, or are you just sitting at your desk so you don't feel guilty? It is much easier to concentrate if you have planned a task to carry out. See page 52

Focus is strongly connected to all the things we have considered so far in this Chapter.

▶ *Motivation*
▶ *Commitment*
▶ *Relaxation*

All help you focus.

Concentration is an important aspect of focus. Concentration is affected by:

▶ *Where you study*
▶ *When you study*
▶ *How you study*

We will be going on to consider all these things now.

It is important for you to know what helps you to concentrate and what disturbs your concentration.

You may find it helpful to work through the concentration checklist to the right and complete the exercise below.

Your concentration

List five things that …

Stop you concentrating

Help you to concentrate

Place

Where?

As we touched on in the first Chapter, if you are training to be an accountant, then it is probable that you are learning in more than one location.

You are undertaking *practical training* at your office. You are probably being given *teaching* at a college or training company.

Lastly, and importantly in this book, you will be *studying privately* and trying to learn the mechanics of what you have been taught and have experienced.

The 'Where?' in this book is going to largely concentrate on the question of where you would be best advised to study privately, as the questions of where you are taught, and where you receive practical training will largely be decided for you.

'Where?' is a difficult question to address in a book for the following reasons:

- Everyone's circumstances are different
- Generalisations can be unhelpful
- It is a matter of personal preference
- It may be a matter you feel you have little control over

However, think through the following issues:

1 Honesty. Own up if you know you study in a place which is not conducive to study for any reason (you don't really want to study/you get lonely studying when everyone else is having fun/it is more comfortable on the bed...)

2 Choice. You may not think that you have many choices about where you can study, but look at the list of options you could consider (given below).

3 Relaxation and balance. Remember that the tense brain is uncooperative, so study in a place where you can relax (just remember to be honest about the balance between relaxation and concentration.) For example, if you hate libraries, don't make yourself go to one...

Study options

Some of these may be silly, but what about:

Public library, local café in its quiet period, local cricket match, the attic, granny's front room, a spare room at your college, the park, your office after everyone's gone home/got in, local church, late night trains, local curry house before 11.30 pm

It depends what you are trying to get away from...

I find

I used to work in front of the telly when I really didn't want to be working. This was a lose-lose situation, because I neither watched the telly properly, nor got any work done. If you recognise yourself doing this, compromise. Do an hour's work in quiet instead of two in front of the box. Then watch the programme.

College

If you want to find a quiet place to study, your office has a 24 hour culture and it's not easy to find a quiet corner at home, have you considered whether it would be possible for you to study before or after hours at your college?

Ask the following questions:

1 **Is it possible that I could stay after class and make use of the room?**

2 **What hours is the college open?**

3 **If not, is there another room or a library I could use?**

4 **Does anyone mind if I do that, and should I let anyone know I am here?**

Library

Unless where you live is very remote, you probably have access to a public library. This is another place that you can consider taking your study too.

However, public libraries aren't always everyone's cup of tea. They can be noisy, and they do not always come fitted with desks and places to study unless they are in big cities.

There may be other options.

The association you are training to be a member of may have a library.

Alternatively . . .

Is there a library at your office?

This probably only applies to larger firms, but if there is one, make sure you make full use of it, if you want to vary the place where you study.

Your office

Your office is probably plentifully supplied with large desks. What a shame that they go to waste for certain hours in every 24. **Study the culture of your office or department and consider whether you could make use of your office as a place of study**. It may be that everyone works late, but no one comes in before 9am. Could you bear to get up an hour earlier to come in and get some study done before anyone else is there? (Check what time the building opens first!) Alternatively, it may have an early culture, but there are always some desks free in a quiet area by 5.30pm. Could you bear to stay for an hour or so and take advantage of this solicitude?

An advantage of studying at work if you can is that there is a clear distinction between where you work (work) and where you relax (home).

49

Home

Everyone's home is different and will have different features and spaces for you to put yourself in. But here are some ideas:

Desk

As you will be studying from Study texts and files, you need a **flat space** on which to work.

In order for you to be able to spread out your work so that you have room to manoeuvre and not spill your cup of coffee, ideally your flat space should also be quite **sizeable**.

It has been suggested that reading is facilitated by the book being propped up at a **30 degree angle**. Desks which incorporate such a feature are expensive, and you may be able to manufacture something similar - using other books to prop things up, or by investing in a book rest (you can buy them in kitchen shops) which look rather like a music stand.

You will also require flat space to write on, when trying questions.

You are likely to have invested in a number of texts and create some files. **Shelves are likely to be a necessity.**

Attic

Having a loft conversion is probably beyond your pocket, but if you are desperate for peace and quiet, give your

Study

This is a fantastic number one place to study, if you can use it whenever you like and it's not filled with someone else's work. It is probably also the room most unlikely to exist in most people's houses.

If you do have a study, set yourself up a desk and shelving, create an atmosphere which relaxes you and go for it!

Kitchen

It is probably less than ideal to work in a kitchen. The table might be nice and big, but there are too many potential distractions. You may feel tempted to stop working and start eating or drinking, and food and drink are easily accessible in the kitchen.

It is also a place where other people are likely to go if you don't live alone. Someone will need to cook the dinner, or your flatmates will want to get beer out of the fridge…

Which room?

Think through the key factors:

Are you alone?

(cont)
roof some consideration. Is there unused space up there you could board up and fill with a desk?

Bedroom

If you are living at your parent's home, or lodging with someone, this may be your best option. Is there room for a desk in your room? If not, you may find that, although pricey, an investment in some space saving furniture may pay dividends. For example, the IKEA* catalogue contains some ideas such as 'loft beds'. You may like to work in bed, and while previously we have advised you to work where you are relaxed and comfortable, it may not be advisable to work in bed. If trying to write (and, as we shall discuss in Chapter 4, this will be necessary) you are likely to get uncomfortable and this will break your concentration and encourage you to stop.

Living room

The living room may be a good place to work if there is room for a table. However, it is also a room in which people socialise, and this may not be at one with your need to concentrate and study. Be honest with yourself. Are you really going to concentrate on economics or financial decisions while your friends/family/flatmates are watching Eastenders? Are they going to appreciate you trying to?

If you do try and work in a living room, you are going to have to be very disciplined in your approach to your work, and also considerate to anyone who is trying to use the room for its proper purpose.

Have you got enough space?

Do you have a desk?

* BPP should point out, of course, that they don't hold shares in IKEA. The authors just shop there sometimes . . .

Ambience

> *The question of 'how' to approach your studies,* that is, the type of study skills you will require, is looked at in Chapter 4, Study Skills.
>
> The question 'how?' in this Chapter is really *an extension of the question 'where?'*. It is still looking at the environment in which you are going to study, but looks at peripheral things, such as the walls you are looking at, your movement during study, the temperature in your room, the things you can hear.
>
> These may not seem as important as the question of where you study, but they are. And in actual fact, *they will probably impact significantly on how you choose the place you study* - remember how we said you might not want to work in the kitchen, because of various peripheral things, such as movement, people and heat?

How?

Scholars and educators will debate the relevance and importance of things that we are going to look at in the next few pages.

In our opinion, these things are only as important as they seem to be to you. If they matter to you, get them right!

Over the next few pages we are going to make a few comments on how seemingly peripheral things may impact on your studies, in a good or bad way. We have already noted a few of them in our observations about concentration, and it is in that context that we revisit them here. The golden question is always: 'Does it adversely affect your concentration?' If the answer is yes, get rid of it!

In the past, there have been some rules about study, such as, 'you must study in silence'. We may invite you to break the rules, if you can honestly say that you are creating a study system for you that works.

What are we going to look at?

Temperature   **Company**
Vision   **Noise**

Intention

We have mentioned intention before. Do not cheat yourself. To study effectively (and probably more efficiently) you have to approach your study sessions honestly, with an intention of trying to learn.

Sound

People are usually divided on the question of whether silence when you study is a good idea. As ever, we think whatever honestly works for you is the best policy.

It is a good idea to distinguish between planned and unplanned noise, however. Unplanned noise, such as drills in the street, a car alarm, a clock ticking, can be very irritating, and will affect your concentration.

We advise: Take a quick look around your room before you start work and eliminate any potential sources of irritating noise before you start. You should also take a quick look out of the window. If workmen are massing, can you go and work at the back of the house?

However, planned noise, particularly music, may have a beneficial effect on your study. Experts have shown that a quality in Baroque music has a particularly beneficial effect on the brain, relaxing the brain to an optimum level. You obviously have to work within your own taste, though.

I find

Music helps me to relax into my study. However, I always know when it is not working, because I find that once I am concentrating, I can no longer hear the music - so if I can hear it, I'm not!.

Once I hear the music, I need to take a break.

Some people who are musical may find that playing music helps them to remember facts, because they associate the facts with the music in their head. Remember that you are not actually going to be able to listen to music in the exam, though.

Vision

Your sense of sight is one of your more commonly used senses.

If your eyes are tired from reading, or from looking at your own handwriting, they will be prone to distraction by things around them.

It is important to consider what you can see from your place of study, and to further consider whether it will distract you.

Some people would advise you to sit in front of a blank wall in a relaxing colour (ie not fiery red), or a beautiful scene. Some would keep the motivation statement we suggested on page 44 in front of them to look at if their attention wandered.

You know what distracts you. If it is a window, don't study next to one, etc ...

Temperature

People can generally tell you whether they like working in hot or cold temperatures. I prefer cold, **what do you prefer?** Then when you sit down to study, make sure the temperature is right.

Another important factor is **changes in temperature**. This is likely to be distracting. **If you can control the temperature, do**. Make sure the window is open/closed before you start, turn the radiator up or down. If you leave it, you may use it as an excuse to wander away from your study ...

Company

If you live alone, this may not be an issue which affects you unduly. For those who live with friends or family, company when studying can be a significant problem.

On the flip side of the coin, the company of people undertaking the same process as you can be very useful. Later we shall review the helpfulness of teaching in order to learn. As part of that, discussing issues arising from your study with a person who is also learning can be a helpful review, and an indicator of any problems that might have arisen.

Friends and family

Friends and family can be **extremely helpful** when you are studying accountancy (for example on those nights when you have three hours worth of study to do in one and a half hours and you haven't eaten all day, and someone has put the dinner on the table so you don't have to cook it yourself ...).

They can also be **extremely unhelpful**.

When you study, you will be seeking to **concentrate** on your work, and **avoiding distractions** which may take away from that concentration.

Friends can be extremely distracting. Unless you have very considerate friends, or friends who are in the same boat as you, friends may not understand why that person who used to be the life and soul of the party is now always found with their head in a book.

If you live with your friends, you might also find that they are very **noisy**. They might not mind being evicted sometimes, but will not be too keen on you asking them to keep it down all the time in their own home.

You need to strike a balance. You need to **explain** your position to people from the outset. You need to consider options such as **studying away from home on occasion** (at work, or in a library), investing in some **ear plugs**, and scheduling **guilt-free nights** out with your friends so that you don't turn into a complete hermit!

Study partners

The phrase **'study buddy'** may throw you into a tremendous squirm. However, if you can get over your squeamishness, you may find that discussing your study with someone else who is studying is a **very useful tool.**

Time

When?

In the next few pages we are going to address the question of When? We shall look at time. For the next three or four years, you may make some of the following observations:

> **There aren't enough hours in the day.**
>
> **Where has the last year gone?**
>
> **I have plenty of time until my exams ... whoops, where did it all go?**
>
> **I don't have time to do all the study I have to do this week.**
>
> **My manager doesn't understand. I've got a course exam next week, I can't possibly work overtime.**

You are going to have to learn to be **creative with time**.

Whatever your normal preference with regard to organising yourself is, to succeed in studying accountancy, you should learn how to **timetable** and **plan your time**. This does not have to be a formal process, but it can be if it helps.

The questions that you will have to find answers to with regard to your studying are these:

- *When should I study?*
- *How frequently?*
- *How long for?*

*There are some **general answers** to these questions, but all of them **must be adapted for personal style and practice**.*

*As always in this book, the aim is for you to **observe yourself** and work out **what is best for you**. On the next page there is a mini questionnaire to get you thinking about your study in terms of time. See what you discover about yourself and then try and **apply your own pattern to some of the suggestions we make**.*

*Remember that **honesty** is the best policy as usual. Can you really complete these exams taking the approach you favour, or should you adapt your style?*

Fleeting time • • •

Think about how you have studied in the past and in particular, to what time frame you have studied. Would you sum yourself up as 'Last minute wonder' or 'Slow and steady wins racer'?

Please assess whether the following statements reflect your approach, using (1) as 'strongly reflects my approach' and (5) as 'does not reflect my approach' and (2) to (4) as degrees between these two positions.

	Statement	(1)	(2)	(3)	(4)	(5)
1	I plan my work.	☐	☐	☐	☐	☐
2	My plans contain specific time deadlines.	☐	☐	☐	☐	☐
3	My plans incorporate time off from study.	☐	☐	☐	☐	☐
4	I never plan.	☐	☐	☐	☐	☐
5	I get to the week before exams and then spend a lot of time planning.	☐	☐	☐	☐	☐
6	I plan as a device to stop me starting working.	☐	☐	☐	☐	☐
7	I always plan 'lack of understanding gaps'.	☐	☐	☐	☐	☐
8	I don't plan initial work but always plan revision.	☐	☐	☐	☐	☐
9	I find plans constrictive because I don't know how I will respond to different topics.	☐	☐	☐	☐	☐
10	I think planning is a waste of time.	☐	☐	☐	☐	☐
11	I like to study for short periods, regularly.	☐	☐	☐	☐	☐
12	I like to save my effort for one big session.	☐	☐	☐	☐	☐
13	I prefer to work in the morning.	☐	☐	☐	☐	☐
14	I prefer to work in the evening.	☐	☐	☐	☐	☐
15	I can only work after midnight.	☐	☐	☐	☐	☐
16	I take lots of breaks.	☐	☐	☐	☐	☐
17	I can't study for two days in a row.	☐	☐	☐	☐	☐
18	I like to have a good run at work - do it for a week solid and then ignore it.	☐	☐	☐	☐	☐
19	I find it impossible to sit down and work unless the exams are looming.	☐	☐	☐	☐	☐
20	I find I go off like a train, but by the time the exams come round, I've forgotten it all.	☐	☐	☐	☐	☐

Analysis

You may not have needed the questionnaire to analyse your study style, but if it is a while since you last studied, a little prompting won't have hurt. Use the matrix below to analyse how you study.

What is your attitude to planning and timetabling your work?

When do you like to work?

... In a day?

... In a course?

Be prepared to change • • •

One thing that this book is trying to do is get you to approach your studies in a way that it **tailor made** both **to you** and to **accountancy training**.

The best way to approach this set of learning may not be the same as approaches you took to other things in the past, even if (a) that approach worked well in those circumstances, and (b) you have previously studied accountancy in some form, eg at university. You **may have to be prepared to change**, or **to adapt your style** to meet the challenges that this training has in store.

*Studying accountancy will be **different** to any other studying you have done before, although it will have similarities. You will have attended school, and may have attended university. Be prepared for the fact that this new venture will not be the same.*

*The key differences are that **studying accountancy often runs alongside having a full time job**, so you will be receiving 'snatches' of teaching along the way.*

*Your own private study will impinge upon your own time in a way that it is unlikely to have done before, **you must be prepared to make time to study**.*

*The syllabuses for professional exams are **far reaching and extensive**, despite the time constraints on those studying for the exams, so be prepared to work hard.*

When?

The question of 'when?' will be strongly influenced by the method of teaching you choose or your firm buys for you. This may be a classroom course, or a course of Home Study.

BPP offers various types of courses for the differing professional qualification (not all courses will be available for each qualification, if you are interested in attending a BPP course, please visit the BPP website at www.bpp.com). The key types of course are outlined here, and the question of 'when?' shall be applied to each of them in the following pages.

Split intensive tuition This incorporates 12 weeks of teaching into two blocks.

Link tuition Under this method, students would receive a no. of single weeks blocks of teaching over a 9 month period.

Block release Where students receive teaching in blocks of 1-5 days over a period.

Day release This allows students to receive teaching for one day a week over a period (which varies according to the course: 12 weeks - 36 weeks).

Evening courses Where students receive teaching for two nights a week over a certain period.

Weekend/Friday-Saturday courses Where students receive teaching for one/two days/weekend over a period.

Question 1

On this page and the next two, we are seeking to answer the first time question:

'WHEN?'

Even if you are attending classroom courses, it will always be necessary for you to undertake some work of your own - see our following up suggestions on the next page.

If you are using a BPP Home Study (distance learning) package, you will receive a detailed study guide, suggesting 'lessons' for you to undertake over time. You will also be given a timetable advising you when you undertake the various elements of the course. So BPP answer lots of the questions for you. You still need to consider when is best for you in terms of your daily schedule (am/pm?), your commitments to work or family and things like your holidays.

If you are going on a period of intensive block tuition, then you are likely to have a period of four or five months directed at study. While you are attending the classroom course part of the time, the tutors will direct you towards question practice. They will also provide suggestions about how to use the time if you have a 'break' period between the two blocks. You should plan how you use this time, and ask the relevant /when/ questions: am/pm?, commitments to work and family, holidays.

Under a Link tuition system, you will receive blocks of teaching over a long period of time, separated by months in which you are expected to carry out some home study. Your tutors will give you some guidance over how to best use the times away from college. You should also plan yourself how to use them to your best advantage. These can be the times where you ensure that your understanding of what you have been taught is sound and you can go over areas which you find difficult until you have mastered them. We shall discuss study methods in Chapter 4. Here remember that down periods between courses are opportunities, and apply the 'When?' checklist below.

Home study package

Split intensive tuition

Link tuition

The 'When?' checklist

Do I study better in   the morning / early evening / late evening   — Constrained periods, remember … — my lunch hour?

When am I planning to go on holiday? — Not just before exams, preferably!

What family commitments do I have which will affect my study? — Putting the kids to bed, granny's 90th birthday weekend, weddings …

Can I take unpaid study leave?

The teaching programmes outlined on this page are similar to the Link method in that you will receive a short burst of teaching and then have a period where you do not have any teaching. Your tutors will direct you about how best to use your time, but remember to use the time wisely to progress your understanding.

Block release

Block release courses are similar to the split intensive tuition discussed on the previous page. It will be important for you to consider the when checklist as to how you are going to link your periods of teaching by your private study, so as to maximise the potential of the periods when you are not at college.

Day release

Day release gives you one day's teaching a week over a period of several weeks. Your tutors will guide you, but ensure that you use the time between courses to clarify your understanding and undertake any work on the days when you are not at college, we advise that you give thought to sectioning a bit of your weekend to devote to study. You might also want to consider allocating it a weeknight. You may find that it is not productive to study on the night of the day you have attended college.

Evening

If you are attending evening courses, then it is likely that you are working in the day time, so will have to keep your private study to other evenings and the weekends. If you are already at college two evenings a week, you might find using other evenings a strain. Perhaps allocating a portion of your weekend to study might be your best option.

Weekend courses

If you attend courses at weekends, the converse is true. You may have to allocate weeknights to following up your study and doing any work which your tutors have suggested. You will probably need to rest on the one day of the weekend you are not attending a course, if you work in the week.

Following up classroom teaching

We would add this general advice ...

> Your tutors will advise you what work would be advisable between your attendance at BPP courses

In the 24 hours following a class, ensure that you just run through the things you were taught and check that nothing came up that you really didn't understand. If such things did arise, make a note of them. You can then take one of the following actions: **(1) Ask, (2) Review in detail in your own study programme, (3) Mixture of both**. If you leave this process too long, you may find that you forget what you didn't understand until much nearer the exams, when you may not have the time to process your understanding.

How frequently?

> **Scientists have discovered that the brain is more likely to remember something if it is exposed to that thing frequently over a time period.**

Your brain is more likely to recall the things you have been taught and have learned for your exam, if you expose your brain to it more than once. You are likely to have a study technique that exposes your brain to things at least twice: the first time when you gain or receive the information, and your revision time.

Experts on the brain would suggest that you should expose your brain to information at least six times. You could use the classroom follow up as another exposure, but might want to build more such recall exposures in to your week. That may mean if you are attending a weekly course that you look over the things you learned on a course three or four times between classes. This may not be a long process by the third or fourth time, don't worry. If there is a long time between your first class and the exam, you might want to spread your recall exposures over that time period. However, the first few reviews should be close together.

Building blocks

The other important consideration is that your study is set up like a set of building blocks. Something you are taught on one course, or you read in one study session is likely to underpin something you will meet in a future session.

Therefore, if your understanding of the foundations is limited, you will not be able to place the later blocks on your pile of learning. This may adversely affect your later performance.

Building blocks • • •

Two things impact upon the question of how frequently, in addition to all the practical issues which we have raised when considering 'When?'.

The first is the review theory, which considers your brain recalls material. This will be important to you as you sit the exam hall, you can be sure of that!

The second is the way that your teaching is set up, both teaching you receive on classroom courses and the teaching you receive from BPP Study Texts. We shall call this the building blocks theory.

Review things frequently to ensure that gaps are filled

How long?

The question of how long will also be answered in part by the practical restraints on your time. You may have brief 'windows of opportunity', for example, your lunch hour or at 6 o'clock on Wednesday before swimming. In these instances, 'how long?' is answered for you - as long as you've got.

At other times, you may find that you have a choice. You may have allocated a whole Saturday to study, or an entire evening. It is then important to plan how long you intend to study for and what breaks you intend to take.

So here is another interesting insight into recall for you ...

Recall: primacy and recency

Study period one

Study period two

The diagram above shows two study sessions of the same length of time. The study period is illustrated in each case by the green block.

In the first study period, the student took no breaks. In the second, the student took four. Breaks are shown by the curved line being broken.

The diagram illustrates the concepts of primacy (you recall what happened first) and recency (you recall what happened most recently) - when the brain remembers best...

The brain recalls more easily things that you learn at a beginning or end of a session

To prove this, try and memorise a list of items, and analyse the result. You will recall a higher number of items at the beginning and end of each list.

Recall is shown in the diagram by the curved line. In study period one, the student recalls things more strongly from the start and end of the session (shown by the arrows). This is also true in study period, but they also recall things better from before and after each break which they took.

The outlook is good

Breaks are our friends, and we are positively encouraged to indulge.

But always remember:

You must approach your study honestly. Taking breaks every five minutes because you don't really want to be studying at all will adversely affect your concentration. In other words, there won't be anything to recall! Take breaks sensibly and honestly

Also remember the important of **reviewing** the material, particularly that which is in the **recall dips**.

Study skills

- Learning styles
- Types of subject
- Study environment
- Study skills
- Revision
- Types of question
- Exam paper

Study skills

Points made so far ...

Teaching and learning are not the same thing.

A variety of skills are required to pass accountancy exams.

BUT ...

Don't let studying drive you mad!

This Chapter should help you create an effective approach.

The question of how to go about it may seem unanswerable! Be reassured; that is why this Chapter is here.

This Chapter looks at a variety of study skills and, as discussed to the right, invites you to consider what methods suit you best. It will consider both types of information provision that are common in accountancy studies, lectures and home study. It is important for you to convert teaching into learning.

Another important piece of advice that this Chapter will give you is to think about the subject you are looking at before you dive in. In Chapter 2, the types of subject you will be studying were discussed. It is unlikely that you should approach them all in the same way. Tailor your approach…

Link

Remember back in Chapter 1, we discussed *learning styles*. Hopefully you worked through the illustrations that you were given there, and learnt a little about *how you prefer to study*.

This is the Chapter where that *self-awareness* will be the most useful, so you might want to *flick back* and *remind yourself* what you learnt.

Remember as you work through this Chapter, that knowing you *have two objectives to*:

1. *Discover* learning methods that suit you best and will facilitate your accountancy studies.

2. *Identify* study skills you do not like or find easy and try to *develop* them if necessary.

Chapter key

As this Chapter is closely linked with the learning styles Chapter, the following references are given when a skill is especially suited to a particular style.

Linguistic

Maths/logic

Spatial/visual

Musical

Interpersonal

Intrapersonal

Bodily kinaesthetic

Two stages of skills

*The diagram shows a **brief outline** of the skills that we will be looking at in a great deal more detail in the rest of this Chapter.*

*The skills which are included in the **circle** are the same whichever course method you have taken, as they relate to work done after the course. Therefore, we shall deal with the skills relating to attending courses, and then move on to study skills used at home.*

Listening — Following up — Recording — Memory techniques — Practice → **UNDERSTANDING** → **RECALL**

Reading — Following up — Recording — Memory techniques — Practice

Classroom courses / Home study courses

(a) Listening
(b) Recording (1)
(c) Follow up (1)
(d) Reading
(e) Recording
(f) Follow up (2)
(g) Recall
(h) Use

STAGE 1 Classroom / STAGE 2 Home Study

Learning styles

Incidentally, just to ram home our point about learning styles, the diagram above has been produced in two styles. I think that the one on the top will appeal to spatial visual people and the one on the bottom will appeal to maths-logical people.

▶ Do you agree?
▶ Which one do you prefer?

Listening

Listening is an art of concentration. The ear is capable of hearing the noise being made by the tutor, even if there are other noises around, but to actually register what is being said, you have to concentrate.

Test it!

Go to a loud place, like an airport or a football match and try and have a conversation with someone. You will find that you can hear more than you think and that hearing increases as you concentrate.

If you find listening difficult, you might want to try out one or more of the following ideas:

1 ... **Take notes** of what the lecturer is saying. Note taking is discussed on the next page in more detail. You will have to listen in order to write down what is being said.

> **I find ...**
> That I cannot concentrate on lectures at all unless I discipline myself to make notes on what is being said.

2 ... **Tape the lecture** (with permission). Then you can listen to it again or even at your leisure.

3 ... **Practise listening** Borrow some talking books from the library, follow a Parliamentary debate on television…

4 ... **Know what distracts you and avoid it** at lectures (windows, the door, friends, noisy air conditioning units…)

A human person's healthy ear is amazing. We have an incredible capacity to *hear*.

However, as many parents or spouses observe, the capacity to *hear* and the capacity to *listen* are *not the same thing*.

People who noted in Chapter 1 that they were *aural people* will probably not find the skill of listening hard. Others may find that listening for extended periods of time is a chore.

If you are going to be given a lot of information aurally, then it is *important to learn how to listen*, or you may have to do a lot of work twice.

The wonder of hearing

" *I can always hear if my baby is crying, it doesn't matter what else is going on ...* "

" *I always prick my ears up when people are talking about football. It's like I have radar or something ...* "

67

Notetaking

Why take notes?

We touched on one reason to take notes on the previous page. Taking notes forces you to concentrate on what the lecturer is saying. This is one reason I found taking notes particularly helpful.

However, note taking can have the converse effect if you concentrate so hard on note taking that you lose track of what the lecturer is saying, so read the notes to the left to ensure that your note taking is effective.

Another reason is that you can keep the notes for future reference. You cannot 'keep' the lecture in the same way.

Notes can also be an important element of your review process, discussed later.

The beauty of the second icon is that when you re-read the notes that you have made from the lecture and they don't make sense,

(a) YOU WON'T PANIC - they never made sense
(b) YOU KNOW TO ASK SOMEONE - follow up, (see the next page)

What to note down

Unless you know shorthand, you are going to be unable to write down everything that the lecturer says. In any case, to do so would be ineffective and wasteful.

A lecturer will repeat points to reinforce them, will give examples and further examples, will outline the background to topics which you have already covered and will teach you the essential things you need to know on a topic.

You do not need to make a note of most of these things. When making notes on a lecture, you need to note down the key points which the lecturer makes explaining the topic, and any examples that you find helpful.

Your own shorthand

In advance of a lecture, you should decide upon some simple shorthand of your own to save time. Here are two ideas to get you started:

▶ **Abbreviate key words**

This will save you time and make note taking easier.

> **Example**
> Management = mgmt or !

▶ **Use icons**

To highlight in the margin key points which the lecturer has made. You can use multiples of these to distinguish between important and absolutely vital…

To remind yourself of areas which confused you or you found difficult, or you were aware that you didn't understand as you were making the notes.

> **Examples**
>
> *
>
> !

Design your notes

It is also important to think about what your notes look like, because that will affect how you review them and whether you use them properly in future.

Don't try and save paper - space out your notes to make them easier to read. This may involve:

▶ Double spacing your lines
▶ Not writing across the full page
▶ Frequent paragraphing

Use headers and boxes and circles and icons and pictures to identify key points.

Follow up

As we have noted above, these notes are ad hoc notes, written at speed when listening to someone speaking.

You can convert these notes into useful revision material.

Another great beauty of the system is that the conversion process is a review, which is part of the learning process.

(a) **Rewrite the notes** into notes that are coherent and flow properly, omitting any sections that on review seem unnecessary. These notes will become useful revision material.

(b) If you have a few !'s, think them through, or read around the subject to see if you can make them make sense. You may need to make a note to ask your lecturer about them when you next see him/her

(c) If you get to the end of a single lecture and you have lots of exclamation marks in your margin, check immediately what the problem is. There may be several issues, as highlighted here.

"Doesn't this all take too much time - why can't I just listen to the lecture?"

The question above is valid, because as we noted above, it is important not to be so devoted to your notes that you forget to listen to the lecture.

However, deciding in advance to double space your lines will not take time during the lecture and an asterisk only takes a second to scribble.

Try these note taking techniques and you might find that they become a vital part of an effective study system.

Potential causes of lots of !'s

1. You may need some 1 to 1 help on this topic.

2. You may have misunderstood something early which will make everything else make sense.

3. There may have been a problem with the lecture.

Reading

> *If you are a **visual linguistic person**, then it **may** be that you **find reading easy**.*
>
> *Aural bodily kinaesthetic people (random example) may find sitting and reading a book near impossible.*
>
> *Whichever category you fall into, here are a couple of points of interest which may please you:*
>
> 1. **Effective study rarely** requires you to **read** a book **cover to cover**.
>
> 2. **BPP Study Texts** are **tailored** to your syllabus so you **only** have to **read** things that are be **examinable**.

We are going to look at two things:

- The skill of reading
- Approaching study materials

The skill of reading

Reading is like many other skills, it improves with practice. If you hated reading when you were at school, then you probably gave it up to all intents and purposes when you left. Suddenly expecting yourself to be a genius at it again is asking a lot.

Of course, if you have always been a bookworm, you do practice regularly, and you probably could analyse an improvement over time.

Skill in reading is often measured in terms of time. People who think they are bad at reading moan 'I'm really slow.' In terms of reading, this is not necessarily a bad thing, although if you are studying, time is likely to be of the essence. However, the key skill in reading is comprehension. There is not much point reading, if you are not taking the information in…

1 Practise reading (things that interest you …)

Try the following:

- Keep a book or magazine (one with words, not pictures!) next to the toilet to peruse in a spare moment.
- Read all the adverts on the bus, train, tube or billboards on the way to work.
- Read the back of the cereal packet as you eat your breakfast.

Even if you think it's easy ● ● ●

Some people find reading very difficult and this fact can put them off their study even if they have fabulous memories or are otherwise well equipped. Others don't.

Even if you wonder what all the fuss is about, some of the suggestion made here about **how to approach study materials may be useful**.

2 Read out loud

If you find that you struggle to understand what you are reading, and you read things over several times to make sure that you have got them straight, try reading out loud for a little while. You might find that you respond better to hearing the words instead of seeing them.

Of course, reading things out loud often takes longer than reading them in your head, so this won't necessarily help your time management. So it might be best to save this technique for the most complex areas…

3 Read key words

BPP Study Texts are written to be concise, but to be in English, they have to include certain words that aren't necessarily vital.

Test it!

The cat sat on the mat.

If you read the above sentence, you know what the author is getting at. However, you would probably also get the idea if you read the following:

Cat sat mat.   Half of the sentence wasn't vital to your understanding!

It is a particular skill of learning to spot words which aren't vital and not to bother reading them. This will save you time and it will save your eye concentration, but it won't affect your comprehension.

It is a skill that needs practice. It is probably best to practise on less important things than your study, for example a novel when you are on holiday, or the next long memo you get at work…

BPP help you by emboldening some key words in our Study Texts. But before you get over-excited, we certainly wouldn't claim that you can pass the exams by only reading the bold words.

The key words skill

Be discerning in when you apply this skill, however. **Some subjects** (a key example being law, you should think of others) by their nature involve a **need for precision**.

In law an 'and' or an 'or' might be vital.

Approaching study materials

At BPP we pride ourselves on producing study materials which include a number of features to help you read our products in the most effective way possible.

1 Introductory ('roman numerals') pages

NB. The contents page of any book is a useful reference point.

The Introductory pages of a BPP book contain information: about the exam, the contents of the book and also signposts and advice for using the book effectively.

In a BPP Practice & Revision Kit, you are likely to find a revision programme, a question and answer checklist and a topic index showing the questions by topic area.

In a BPP Study Text, you are likely to find the syllabus and study guide. It is helpful to read this - so that your reading is focused to what you need to know. Because this is useful information and it signposts your reading in a chapter, we also put the relevant sections of the syllabus or study guide in the introduction to each chapter in the Text.

2 Introductions and chapter roundups

These are summaries of the chapter, giving you a helpful insight before you dive into the chapter. Knowing in summary what the chapter is about will help your comprehension.

3 Other features

Other features include shaded boxes for key concepts, use of tables to highlight advantages and disadvantages and other visually helpful design features. The books are designed to help reading, by giving your eyes variety and making you aware of the important points, which are presented differently.

4 Text order

We have ordered the text in what we see to be a logical way. But you don't have to follow us! Start with a short topic, or one you already know something about - start on page 346 if you want! The chapter introduction should highlight whether you need to be familiar with other topics to understand this one…

Reading checklist

▶ Read the summary of the chapter in the introduction/chapter roundup to get an overview.
▶ Check the syllabus/study guide so that you are clear on what you are supposed to be learning
▶ Take note of key terms and concepts highlighted in the chapter
▶ Re-read the chapter roundup to ensure that you are clear - if not, go back and re-read

Reading and notetaking

We discussed taking notes from a lecture on pages 68 to 69. Particularly if you are doing Home Study, you may want to take notes from the reading you do.

Much of what was said in those pages is relevant here. It is important that you take notes which you will want to go back to and read, it is important that you signpost to yourself things which are important and things which you find difficult.

However, note taking from reading is not an ad hoc exercise. While the words which the lecturer says have a fleeting quality, the words in a book stay there, so you can take your time. Try the following:

Two stage reading process

Skim read the chapter or section you are focusing on in the study session. This involves maximum use of the key word technique and no re-reading paragraphs.

Then conduct a detailed read through, taking notes as you do so.

The skim should make you aware of what the topic is about and what the key issues are, while the detailed read through with note taking helps you to understand the topic.

Why take notes when reading?

It is not necessary to take notes when using a BPP Study Text, because the key details that you need to know are recorded succinctly for you there, and key points are highlighted.

However, you may want to take notes anyway. This could be for several reasons:

1. To help you to concentrate

2. To note things which strike you as you are reading

3. To highlight areas you find difficult and need to verify with someone

4. As a review exercise (see later).

Use your own words

If you do take notes when reading a book, it is important that **you do not just copy out vast chunks** of it. This may aid your memory of what the book says, but does not aid your comprehension of **what it means**.

When trying to learn and understand topics, if you **make notes in your own words** of what you have read, this shows a **comprehension** of the topic. If you can explain it in your own words, **you understand it.** This is an important step in the learning process.

If you understand a topic at the outset, you will find practice and recall becomes substantially easier at the revision stage. **Revision**, after all, is a **reminder of what you know**, not an opportunity to finally understand all that stuff you read a few weeks or months ago!

Recording
(Maximising the effectiveness of your notes)

The notes you have made as you have attended lectures or read through the Study Text relating to a particular subject will form an important part of your learning. *Your notes belong to you and to you only.*

It doesn't matter what anyone else thinks of them - they are *a means to help you understand and remember the subject for your exam.* Very few people find pages of A4 densely covered in handwriting easy to read.

We mentioned that *design* is important when initially taking your notes. As you work through them and come to revise, you may want to *rehash* your notes again to help you learn from them.

Consider the ideas set out below and on the following page

Cards

BPP produce revision cards called Passcards. These summarise the key points contained within the Study Texts and present them in a visually helpful way.

You may want to rehash your own notes in a similar format, or just use the ones we have put together for you.

Revision cards like this are likely to be useful to **linguistic** people because they are summarised forms of written notes. However, they are also good for **spatial visual** people because the notes have been grouped on the cards in a visually helpful way. A **bodily kinaesthetic** person might find it helpful to produce revision cards because the process of making them (doing it) might help them to remember. The cards present facts in sensible orders for **maths logical** people.

Personal learning style

How you like your notes to be presented is very much a matter of **personal choice**. This is an area where the **impact of learning styles** can be felt strongly.

Think about it

Think about how you like to be presented with information and adapt your notes to meet this need. We have highlighted what we think matches each learning style, but it is **YOUR learning process, YOU decide...**

I find ...

Being a visual person, when I was studying I found poster notes helpful (eg, flow charts showing controls cycles in auditing) which I looked at whenever I went to my fridge, or the front door, or where ever else I had put them.

Maps and posters

BPP use mindmaps in Study Texts to illustrate the syllabus and in places to give an overview of a topic. You can produce similar maps to summarise key topics. A map can be turned into a poster.

These are particularly helpful to **spatial visual** people as they illustrate topics graphically and show the links in a topic. Again, a **bodily kinaesthetic** person may find creating one helpful. If the map uses words rather than pictures, a **linguistic** person may find it useful. As the facts are presented in a logical order again, this method may also help the **maths logical** person.

Tapes

BPP produce cassette tapes to aid with your revision for some professional schemes. You may want to make your own. Tapes are likely to aid aural people.

Musical people might find it helpful to record revision notes set to music and to play them back. Again, the process of making a tape might aid a **bodily kinaesthetic** person. As it is words being recorded, this might also be good for a **linguistic** person.

Videos

For certain professional schemes, BPP produce tutorial videos. You might find it helpful to turn your notes into video as part of your revision process.

As with the tapes, a **musical** person might find it helpful to record notes to music, a **bodily kinaesthetic** person may find making a video helpful (they could 'act out' their notes) and a **linguistic** person might find it helpful to speak out and then hear the words in a different way.

CD-ROMs and Internet

For many papers BPP produce CD-ROMs for teaching and for self-assessment. **Maths logical** people benefit from the clear sequencing and structure of the material. **Spatial visual** people may find CD-ROMs visually stimulating. **Bodily kinaesthetic** people may benefit from the 'hands on' interactivity.

Following up

Follow up has already been briefly touched on in the context of notetaking. It is vital that if you are given information which you do not understand, you seek clarification. You cannot learn accountancy and pass accountancy exams if you do not understand the information that is given to you.

BPP offers a query service to BPP registered students. People who attend classroom courses can always ask their tutors for help. If you are a Home Study student, you will be aware of the telephone and email support systems that BPP offers. Here are some general guidelines:

In class

- ▶ Try and go with what the lecturer advises (whenever, at the end, etc…)
- ▶ Remember, if asking during a lecture, it is courteous to raise your hand.

At breaks

- ▶ If you wait until a break, the lecturer will have more time to answer you. Ask yourself 'is this vital to my understanding of the next two hours?'

Next day

- ▶ If you were to go home and study a little bit, could you answer your own question? In the long run, the added time spent might pay dividends to your own understanding. You can always ask the next day.

"To ask, or not to ask?
That is the question."

During Home Study

How to ... Telephone queries

Ringing up a tutor with a query may seem like the easiest thing in the world, but it too can be made more efficient. Here are some guidelines to maximise efficiency:

1 Make a note of your tutor's name so you can ask for them. (Your query may have to be passed to someone else if your tutor is teaching).

2 Make sure you tell them what you are studying (professional scheme, paper, topic) so that they can tune into your need as fast as possible.

3 Be certain you know what your question is (you may find it helpful to write it down first). A tutor wants to help, but won't have time to just chat generally about a topic.

4 Write down the answer you are given. There is no point in making a query and then forgetting what you have been told a minute later.

How to ... Email queries

The tricks to maximise efficiency in email queries are similar to the telephone ones, particularly steps 2 and 3.

There are some particular benefits to email queries:

1 The key benefit is that **step 4** (write down the answer) is covered automatically. You can keep the email and add it to your notes - but you can't keep a phone call.

2 If you study at night, you can save all your queries to the end of a study session and then email them. You should receive a reply the next day - before your next study session.

You may need an immediate answer so the phone is better. But if not, your tutor might find it more convenient to fit answering an email into their timetable, so choosing this option could make queries more efficient for everyone.

Recall

> *In order to pass exams*, you need to be able to recall what you have learnt. Recall is an important aspect of memory.
>
> We are going to look at three areas which it might help you to think about in this area. The three areas are:
>
> ▶ Review (review, review, review, review…)
>
> ▶ Memory Techniques
>
> ▶ Practice.
>
> We touched on review in Chapter 3, but will revisit it here.
>
> We shall discuss practice briefly in this chapter and will talk more about different kinds of question in Chapter 6.

What's the big deal?

Memory = Retention + Recall

Your mind stores a lot more than you might give it credit for. This is the retention aspect of memory. We can see proof of this in the dreams we have. They may seem random sometimes, but often your mind will replay things which have happened or that you have thought in the day - which you may not have realised that you stored.

> **I find ...**
>
> That in my first year of accountancy studies, I did a lot of work on introduction to financial decisions late into the evening, because I found it very difficult to understand. I often woke up having dreamed about it - so my mind was obviously taking stuff in, even if I didn't understand it!

Recall is vital to your studies as accountancy is examined - that is, you will have to go into an exam hall and produce what you know on a given day and in answer to given questions. If you have all the knowledge in the world tied up in your brain, but cannot get it out on that given day, you will fail your accountancy exams.

There are **five main factors** to recall:

| 1 | Primacy |
| 2 | Recency |

These two were covered in Chapter 3, page 62.

| 3 | Review |

Review was also covered briefly in Chapter 3. We look at it in a more practical way on page 61.

| 4 | Linking |
| 5 | Standing out |

We shall consider the implications of 'linking' and 'standing out' in memory techniques.

Total recall

What is so great about elephants, anyway? **Your** brain is amazing. It has the capacity to remember everything that your syllabus requires of it.

You need to practise remembering, so that on D Day, you can produce your best.

I never forget …

Review

Example Day X of lectures

8 am — **Re-read** a **summary** of yesterday's lectures, or jot one down if you did not complete one in the previous day.

9 am — Lecture begins. **Take notes** as outlined on page x.

10.30 am — At break, get a coffee (of course) but then chat quickly about the lecture with a study partner or friend (ie, swap notes verbally). This establishes whether you are on the same/**right** tracks as one another. (If you are not, ask the tutor who is right.) It also acts as **quick review** of the previous hour and a half.

This step can be repeated three times in the average day of Lectures - apply it according to the pattern of yours.

4.30 pm — Go home. **Take a break** from your studying for a little while. It is important to clear your head after a day sitting in lectures, or you may go mad.

6 pm — Work through the **notes** you have taken in the day - **organise** and **re-write** as necessary as previously discussed. This acts as a further review. Then do any **question practice** directed by your tutors.

10 pm — **Ring mum** and see if you can **explain** to her in 15 minutes what you learnt today. Or, if she's not too interested in debits and credits, you could try explaining them to your teddy bear!

We discussed the concept of review in Chapter 3. As we observed there, experts consider that in order to **maximise retention** *of information, you should* **expose** *your brain to the information you want to retain at least* **six times**.

As a result of this information, you might want to consider a **study system** *such as the one set out on the right hand side of this page. It shows how you can fit at least* **four reviews** *into a* **small period of time.**

You don't have lectures? Try this • •

The spirit of review as outlined above can also be applied to work you have prepared at home. The two stage reading technique is the first stage - the second read is your first review. Then you can **re-read your notes at the end of each study session and at the beginning of the next one** and on **Saturdays.** And you, too, can chat about accountancy to long-suffering Ted at the end of the day…

Memory techniques

Over the next few pages, we are going to look at two further types of memory techniques. (Remember that the review schedules and study timing tricks that we have already looked at are memory techniques themselves.)

You are probably familiar with the two techniques that we are going to look at. One of them is a technique used in most kinds of learning (even the nursery), the mnemonic, the other is mapping.

A mnemonic is

> "a pattern of letters or ideas which aids the memory"

One reason for the popularity of mnemonics is that they can appeal to a large variety of learning styles.

▶   They are comprised of words, so will linguistic people are likely to find them helpful.
▶   They can be set to rhymes, so they may appeal to musical people.
▶   As stated above, they follow a pattern, which maths-logical people will like.
▶   They can incorporate a story, which a spatial-visual person may find easy to picture.

Mnemonics are probably the least helpful to a bodily kinaesthetic person but - DON'T STOP READING - the story created may be adapted to a drama, which a bodily kinaesthetic person might also find useful.

Mnemonics provide the links which our brain likes to use to recall facts. As you will see on the next page, they can link lists of facts with key words, words to stories and events to rhymes.

Want to know more?

Over the next few pages we will expand on these two techniques, so that we can identify whether you will find it useful to incorporate them into your study systems.

Mnemonics

A key example is the **rhyme**, illustrated below, in the example using the months of the year. The facts which are to be learnt are arranged into a short rhyme. The **metre and rhyme make this easier to remember than a list of facts.**

You may remember this one, too:

*In fourteen hundred and ninety-two
Columbus sailed the ocean blue.*

However, mnemonics do not have to rhyme. They can also consist of **stories**, or a sentence which brings to mind the facts you are trying to remember.

The example below shows the sentence spelling out the first letter of the colours of the rainbow. If you ever learnt music, you may have learnt that

'Every good boy deserves fruit'

to remember which notes fell on lines…

Another type of mnemonic is the **list of words** remembered by being attached to a **key word or acronym**. This is the reverse of the rainbow sentence and it is also illustrated below.

You may have used one to remember financial statement assertions:

Completeness
Occurrence
Valuation
Existence
Disclosure/presentation

…famous **mnemonic stories** are more rare, probably because the memory aide is substantially more useful if the story is relevant to you, but the following story could help you remember the 'i before e' rule:

The school bus always picks me (I) up before Emma, unless Catherine is coming. If she is, the bus goes to Emma's after Catherine's house and picks me up later.

It doesn't have to make sense, so long as you remember it.

> You may have found the old rhyme more useful here!

Thirty days hast September,
April, June and November,
All the rest have 31,
Excepting February alone,
For she has 28 days clear
And 29 in each leap year

Richard
Of
York
Gave
Battle
In
Vain

Segregation of duties
Physical
Authorisation and approval
Management

Supervision
Organisation
Arithmetical and accounting
Personnel

The months   The colours of the rainbow   Internal controls

Mnemonics with numbers

Some people find that it is easy to remember things if they number them.

Illustration

We are going to illustrate remembering with numbers three ways by using the following list of Kings. Some of them have numbers of their own, which may complicate or ease the techniques…we shall see.

William the Conqueror	Richard I
William II	John I
Henry I	Henry III
Stephen and Mathilda	Edward I
Henry II	Edward II

We want to remember all the kings and remember the order in which they reigned, which is the first column followed by the second column.

1. Applying simple numbers

Some people would find that the best way for them to remember that list of kings would be simply to number them in order and then count them off against their fingers.

They would write out the following…

1. William the Conqueror
2. William II
3. Henry I
4. Stephen and Mathilda
5. Henry II
6. Richard I
7. John I
8. Henry III
9. Edward I
10. Edward II

And remember the list by linking the number with the name.

Are you one of those people?

2. Linking the number to the name

If that wasn't you, hopefully you are reading on to discover whether numbers are still for you.

You could link the number with the name to build on the previous technique and remember the list.

For example, using the list to the left, you could remember that William the Conquerer is first (number one) because he was the conqueror and he beat everyone else. William II (2) is then easy to remember, because he follows William 1.

Henry rhymes with three, so you could link those that way. As it is the first time Henry has appeared, it must be Henry I. Using a similar rhyming link, 4 has more, ie more than one person - Stephen and Mathilda.

Perhaps you could use a mathematical idea to link Henry II to Five. Five minus Henry's II is three, which rhymes with Henry.

Can you think of links for the rest of them?

3. The number rhyming technique

The last two 'numbery' memory techniques that we are going to look it may seem a little over complex (you may have thought that number 2 was even taking things a bit far…) but they are effective. I was astonished at the results that I came out with after trying them. But you have to be prepared to go wild with your imagination…

The technique takes the numbers which you have applied to your list of facts to be remembered and links a rhyming word with them which it asks you to picture.

For example:

1	One	Bun
2	Two	Shoe
3	Three	Tree
4	Four	Door
5	Five	Jive
6	Six	Sticks
7	Seven	Heaven
8	Eight	Gate
9	Nine	Dine
10	Ten	Hen

Then you apply the picture to the person you are trying to remember, so for example, you might imagine William the Conqueror having a heavy day in battle and then coming in from the battlefield and having a bun for tea. You might imagine that William II was a tiny man with minuscule feet who had to have his shoes made specially for him, and so on…

Can you think of links between the number images and the rest of the kings?

4. Number pictures, without the rhymes

It may be that you like the idea of technique three, but rhymes are not your thing. The technique is adapted to be more visual than rhyming, as is shown in the next example.

1	One	Spear
2	Two	Swan
3	Three	Bottom
4	Four	
5	Five	
6	Six	
7	Seven	
8	Eight	
9	Nine	
10	Ten	

In this case, the associated word is given to the number because of the way that the number looks. So 1 looks a bit like a spear, 2 looks a bit like a swan and 3 looks like a person's behind, etc…

Now picture these words associated with the people. So, William the Conqueror going into battle with his spear, William II at a great feast eating swan, Henry I with an enormous posterior…

Can you complete the table and link the number images to the kings?

Test it!

Choose your favourite technique and see if you can name the ten kings in the correct order.

Mapping

Mapping is another very visual technique which correlates to both the 'linking' and 'standing out' aspects of our memory.

The technique of 'mapping' has various different titles. It is sometimes called mindmapping, or drawing a mindmap, or can be called making a spider-diagram. We have touched on the technique on page 75, as a possible way to build up your notes.

Here we will look at how you create a 'map' and what the benefits of such a map are for your recall.

Key points

A mind map is supposed to sum up a lot of information, indeed whole topics, in a relatively small space. It involves you identifying 'tags' (these can be words, pictures or symbols) which will trigger your memory on a particular topic.

Commonly, mindmaps will grow from a central point, but this does not have to be the case. The mind map might be showing a certain process, so it might grow in a linear fashion. It could be illustrating a concept which builds on itself, and grows more like a tree.

Some examples of mindmaps are set out on the next few pages. Looking at these is probably the best way to familiarise yourself with the topic - but do not assume that this is the only way to create mind-maps.

> Think of a mindmap as being a graphical representation of your thoughts on a subject - and ensure that the finished product reflects the way you perceive what it is that you are trying to remember.

Express yourself

Do not time yourself when it comes to mindmaps. Consider use of **colour**, **typefaces**, **letter case**, **arrows** . . . whatever helps you remember and makes things STAND OUT. Go for it . . .

The elephant mindmap

1. Topic, clearly highlighted in centre and capitals.

2. Key factors – distinguished by circles and lower case from topic

- African
- Indian
- Types
- Gestation
- Reproduction
- Life expectancy
- Features
- **ELEPHANTS**
- Food
- Habitat — Africa
- Famous
- India/Asia
- Plains
- Nellie
- Dumbo
- Jungle

3. Details and sub details – branch out from the key factors.

4. 'Visual' details can be presented graphically.

All features can be varied by the use of colour, different typefaces etc…

---

1. This mindmap grows from a central point.
2. Key factors pan out like spokes from the central point, showing the important things to remember.
3. Details relating to each key factor branch out of those circles.
4. Symbols or pictures can be used to summarise details.

On the following pages, some more examples are given for you to look at. The Olympic mindmap has been drawn by two people, to show you stylistic differences.

The Olympic mindmaps

Mindmap contents:

- **THE OLYMPIC GAMES** (central)
- **History**: Ancient Greece, Modern games, Laurels
- **Quad-annual**: 2000, 2004, 2008, 2012, etc...
- **Track**: 100m, 200m, 400m, 800m, 1,500m, 3,000m, 5,000m, 10,000m, Marathon, Relay, Hurdles, Steeplechase
- **Field**: Shot, Jumps (Long, High, Triple), Javelin, Hammer
- **Pool**: Singles, Relays
- **Other**: Gymnastics, Boats (Sail, Yachts, Rowing), Shooting, Fights (Judo, Boxing)

Analysis

This mindmap also grows from a central point, with key factors ranged around it. It uses a combination of words and symbols to jog the memory. Details to be remembered branch out from the key points, and sub-points branch out from those details.

Analysis

The two olympic mindmaps are quite similar to look at (growing from a central point, sub points, use of pictures to aid memory). You can see the point illustrated here about how two people's minds work differently, this time in subject matter.

The study process mindmap

SUCCESS!

- Sit exam
- Review
- Stay calm
- More question practice
  - Mock exams
- Revise
  - BPP Passcards
  - Revisit notes
  - Mnemonics
  - Maps
- Question practice
  - BPP Practice and Revision Kit
  - Lecture examples
- Review
  - lots of times
  - different methods
- Take notes
  - icons
  - own words
- Join BPP Home Study programme
  - Read BPP Study Text
- Attend a classroom course
  - Listen to BPP lectures

STUDY PROCESS

Analysis

The mindmap to the left is linear, rather than round because it shows a process. The key stages of the study process are shown in cloud shapes to highlight them. Sub-elements are shown branching off. The large coloured arrows show a clear path through the process.

'Success' is shown at the top as the summit of our endeavour and what we are aiming at. The mindmap on the left stems from the central point and is more comprehensive in detail included, showing how you can vary the detail on the mindmap according to its purpose.

Skills developed by question practice

Interpretation of question requirements

Question requirements indicate how much depth and breadth your answer should have, and the style and format you should use. You also will learn the clues given in questions that will determine your approach.

Choosing the right content

Practice will help you understand the right mix of content for your answer. This includes how much theory to include, also how to use factual detail and practical examples to support your answer. You also may see that stating the obvious may gain you marks.

Answer structuring

Structuring your answer poorly may hide the knowledge you have. Question practice shows you how answers should be structured, the right order of points, and how points need to be developed.

Managing your time

The time available to you and the marker is a limited resource. Practice shows you how much you can write in the time; it brings home the importance of allocating your time and prioritising the most important points so that you develop them properly. Practice also makes you think about making your answer easy to mark.

> **Practice (It really does make perfect)**
>
> Practising questions is a vital part of the review process.
>
> Question practice tests what you know, highlighting any gaps in your knowledge that need to be filled.
>
> Question practice acts as an aid to memory. Answering questions means you have to use what you know actively, selecting relevant knowledge and applying it to the requirements of the question. Because you have thought about what you've learnt, you will find it easier to recall in future.
>
> Question practice also helps you develop the other skills discussed in Chapter 2 that you need to pass accountancy exams.

For **higher level papers** in particular you cannot afford to leave question practice until just before the exam. Because it may not be easy to determine how good your answer is, you should ideally have your answers **marked** by a **knowledgeable person**, a tutor or someone doing the course with you. The marker's assessment may highlight points that are not obvious to you, such as a lack of business awareness or over-complex language. You can then work on these skills by background reading or practising explaining theory to a non-accountant.

Different types of subject ...

In Chapter 2, we outlined the various types of subject that you will be studying.

The subjects are very different, and it makes sense that you should not approach them all in the same way, to achieve the best that you can in each of them.

You may already be able to suggest or guess which subjects you will find most easy to handle.

However, if you find out all you can about the nature of each subject, you should be able to tailor your approach in the best way. This may mean practising study skills that don't come naturally to you.

Financial Accounting is largely a practical subject.

You will have to:

1. Understand
2. **Do**

> This is likely to be good news for **bodily kinaesthetic** people

In the exam, you are likely to have requirements like 'Prepare a cash flow statement in accordance with FRS 1' or 'Produce the consolidated cash flow statement'. This means that practising doing these things is essential.

Law is a theoretical subject.

You will have to:

1. Understand
2. **Explain** or **Apply**

> This is likely to be good news for **maths logical** people

In the exam you are likely to be given a scenario and asked 'What is X's legal position?' This means that practising to think through a situation logically, applying legal rules is vital.

Sherlock

Basically we are suggesting that a **key study skill** is the power to investigate how to approach the subject, before you dive in ...

You can do this by asking someone who knows or by reading the introduction or introductory chapter of your Study Text.

Revision

The last few weeks

This chapter is about the period leading up to your exams and how you should approach revision.

What not to do

If you just set out with the intention of 'revising everything before the exam':

▶ Your revision will be superficial; you will not have spent enough time revising actively, or

▶ You will run out of time, and find that you have not covered important topics

Your time is a limited resource. You must approach revision methodically. Organising your revision involves taking certain key decisions.

What to revise

When to revise

How to revise

Remember!

Revision is the culmination of the continuous review of your material that we discussed in chapter 4.

Be selective!

A vital exam skill in all subjects at all levels is being able to select from what you know about a subject what you need to answer a question. Identification of what is important (what you will need to answer questions) is an essential part of your revision.

Timetable

Remember the revision timetables that you have used for school or university exams in the past and jot down an example. If you have never prepared a revision timetable before, try now to think about what it should contain.

When

Overall timetable

*At the start of your revision period, you should draw up an overall timetable to make sure you cover for **every** paper:*

- All the **most significant topics**
- **Enough other topics**

You also should give thought to:

- **Order.** You may wish to tackle the most important topics first.
- **Skills.** You need to practice key skills, (analysis, communication).
- **Revision course.** Your timetable should fit around what you are doing on the course.
- **Final stages.** You should allow time at the end to sit mock exams and re-read passcards.

Daily timetables

*Having completed an overall timetable, you should draw up **weekly** and **daily** timetables. You should avoid falling far behind your overall timetable; however you should build in **flexibility** if certain topics need more revision than first planned.*

Our timetable

Our revision timetable has the following features.

1 Time
The timings depend on you; you may start with an hour's revision before breakfast or finishing the day by tackling a full exam question from the kit.

2 Subjects
Revising different subjects during the day can keep you mentally fresh. In our timetable law revision after lunch contrasts with spending the rest of the day on financial accounting.

3 Comments
Writing down why you're revising a subject forces you to think about what aspects are the most important.

4 Method
Full exam questions are alternated with shorter exercises focusing on knowledge and question approach.

5 Points forward
These are points you would incorporate into your timetables for future days.

6 Breaks
Breaks are marked for coffee, tea, lunch and dog walking.

Having talked about how you should divide your time up, we are going to move on to consider which subjects you should spend the **most time** revising.

Revision timetable - Saturday 11 June

Time	Subject	Comments	Method	Pts forward
9.00	Statement of Principles	Possible question on basic principles	Read chapter summary/passcard List main principles without notes Read article in April's student magazine	Attempt part question in 3 days time
10.00	Coffee			
10.15 Coffee 11.15 - 11.30	Group accounts	Certain compulsory question per examiner guidance	Questions 39, 42 revision kit - full questions	Ran out of time; accounting for minority interests problems Consult tutor Do another question
12.30	Lunch			
1.30	Unfair dismissal	Certain MCQ/ Probable optional question	Chapter 10 text quick quiz Q63 revision kit - answer plan	Satisfactory. Read passcard and listen to success tape in days before exam
2.30	Tea			
2.45	Cash flow statement	Possible compulsory question, full single company CFS	Q65 revision kit - full question	Included non-cash expenses, test self on common non-cash expenses (Text p100) on Friday
3.45	Tea			
4.00	Statutory accounts proformas	Likely compulsory question; missed out elements of profit and loss a/c previously	Write out proformas	100% correct; try again in a week's time.
5.00	Walk dog			

Evening sessions

Much of your revision may be done in the evenings. Most of the points we make opposite apply to evening revision as well, particularly revising different subjects in different ways and taking short breaks between each session.

What (1)?

Don't forget...

Often students forget to revise certain essentials that are vital when answering exam questions:

Key terms

Report formats

Computation layouts

Basic principles

Strengths

Even if you feel happy with a topic, you must test yourself to see if you are as good at it as you think you are.

A lot of learning can be a dangerous thing

For higher level papers, it's easy to spend too much time revising basic factual knowledge, cluttering your mind with excessive detail. You should spend most time practising *questions; the facts you learn should be those you are most likely to use to support your analysis or argument.*

Key topics

At the start of your revision you should draw up a list of the key topics for each paper. You can identify the important topics in various ways.

- ▶ Recur regularly on the paper.
- ▶ Underlie whole paper (e.g. qualities of information)
- ▶ Often the subject of compulsory questions
- ▶ Current issues
- ▶ Subject of recent articles by examiner
- ▶ Shown as high priority in text/home study material
- ▶ Key * points made by lecturer
- ▶ Tutor tips

These are the areas where you should spend most time, topics on which you need to practise full questions. Remember to cover all examinable aspects of a topic; for example as well as revising a technique, don't forget to revise the weaknesses of that technique.

Be careful…

of over-revising, spending too much time on a topic. You can avoid this by assessing what is the maximum that a question about the topic would ask.

Tips

Treat tips with caution. Some tutors will tip all significant topics; others will hedge their tips with considerable reservations.

It's important to understand **why** a subject has been tipped. A tip on the basis that the examiner has written an article stressing the topic's importance is stronger than a tip that the subject has not been examined for three years 'and is bound to come up sooner or later.'

What (2)?

Difficult areas

Hopefully some topics you found difficult to start with will seem easier when you come to revise them. However there may be some areas where you still lack confidence.

- ▶ You just 'don't like' the area; you find it dull or can't see the point of it.
- ▶ You highlighted the subject as an difficult (!) subject when taking notes.
- ▶ You noted problems when you answered questions or when you reviewed the material.

Having identified problem areas, you need to decide what to do about them. We make some suggestions opposite and will discuss how to revise actively later in this chapter.

Stay positive

Don't get depressed that you have identified an area as difficult; remember instead that you are doing something about it. Other students will have found the same topic difficult and given up.

Don't get bogged down

You should also focus on what is most important about the area, what is likely to earn you the most marks. Don't spend a lot of time trying to understand a complication which will only be worth two marks at maximum in the exam.

Lack of knowledge

If your problem is a failure of knowledge, concentrate on methods that test knowledge such as writing out summaries, quick quizzes and MCQs

Computations

If you struggle with computations, go back to the examples in the text, noting the logic behind each stage. Then practice a question from the kit, referring back to the text if you struggle. Having noted your problems, do a second question without referring to the text, and assess why your performance has differed from the question where you did refer to the text.

Higher skills

If you've had problems with questions involving higher level skills, full question practice will give you more confidence in applying those skills. Write down as part of your plan your previous weaknesses and whilst you're answering the question, constantly remind yourself of them - are you saying enough about why the figures in the accounts have changed? Are your recommendations clear and specific?

Do ask!

Above all don't be afraid to seek help. Maybe someone you know had similar difficulties, was able to overcome them and can help you deal with the problems.

What? (3)

> **Quick revision challenge**
>
> *When you have read the rest of this chapter, jot down some thoughts on how you could revise a particular subject area quickly, but effectively enough to make an attempt at a question on it.*
>
> *Your attempt may be insufficient to achieve a pass on that question, but it may contribute enough marks to help you pass the paper.*
>
> **Our suggestions are shown on the second last page of this chapter.**

And the rest?

We have discussed how you select areas which need a lot of attention when you revise.

However…

You also need to consider whether your revision has sufficient breadth, whether you are revising enough subjects.

Breadth of revision is particularly important on certain types of paper.

▶   Many lower level exams consist partly or wholly of compulsory MCQs/short answer questions which cover all major areas of the syllabus.

▶   With higher level papers containing a mixture of compulsory and optional questions, the topics covered by compulsory questions may be unpredictable.

One check that you can use is to look over exam papers for the last few years in your revision kit. You can check that following your revision plan would have enabled you to answer all of the compulsory questions and sufficient optional questions on each paper.

Remember however that although you need to cover a good breadth of subjects, you should not spend equal time on each.

Past omissions

Old examiner's reports can provide clues on areas that many candidates did not revise at all. These areas are **very tempting** for examiners.

How?

Look at the definitions of revising given below. Some key words have been emboldened. These key words are going to point us in the direction of how we should revise.

A Verb

Remember when you were in Primary school and you were first taught all this stuff? What is verb? - a **DOING** word.

You must be **active** in your revision.

B Examine

Revision is not a process of casting an eye over things - rather a process of looking **carefully**. The examiner is going to examine what you know - **you** need to **get in first**.

C Reconsider

Think things through again. At the end of the course, you will be able to **see links** and connections and it will all begin to make sense as a **coherent** body of information.

C Improve one's knowledge

Remember, revision is an **enhancing process**. We are going to take what you have learnt and make it exam sized and shaped.

E Re-read/look at again

As you will see in the next pages, we do not want you just to read - but you must be sure that in your revision phase it is **genuinely second time** around. If there are areas you have not covered - cover them before you start.

One thing that has been emphasised in this book so far is the need for you to be proactive in your approach to study.

When it comes to revision, we still want you to be proactive, but we also want you to get interactive. Passive revision is not going to be effective.

How you revise is really up to you. You are likely to have done it before, so you probably have some tried and tested methods.

But read through the next few pages, so that you can be critical about your methods, and perhaps enhance your skills.

To revise

A Verb. 1. **B Examine** and improve or amend, **C reconsider** and alter

A Verb. 2. **E Reread work done previously** to **D improve one's knowledge,** typically for an examination

It derives from the French **E** 'to **look at again**'.

Revision pie chart

To the right is a very simple pie chart showing four stages of revision.

*Once you have achieved your planning and know **what** you want to revise and **when** you are going to do it, you need to know **how to...***

*You may have methods which work well for you, but you might want to consider the **reasons** behind the four stage plan, and assess whether you want to incorporate the four stage plan into your personal revision methods.*

Many of the techniques used are going to be microcosms of the study skills set out in Chapter 4.

1. Write it
2. Read it
3. Teach it
4. Do it

Four step revision programme

In the next pages we are going to point out some **benefits** of each of the four stages and also look at some tips and ideas for **how to** do each stage.

Write it!

Tips

1 The revision notes do not have to be predominantly in words - although this will partly be driven by the topics you are revising.

2 Many people find that transferring their notes onto A5 cards is a useful exercise - the cards are manageable and more user friendly than big A4 sheets.

3 Visual people may find that they can visualise particular revision cards - particularly if they have designed the cards to assist that process:

- **Assign a colour code to particular topics**
- **Use icons to highlight important or difficult points**
- **Write key rules or definitions in capital letters**

Why?

Your course notes and own notes are *too bulky* to revise from. You must *create a master set* of notes which *summarise* the key points.

The *act of writing* is a review - and *will help you to remember* the things which you are writing down.

Passcards

BPP have completed step 1 for you, if you are short of time or paper...

Our handy pocket-sized passcards contain exam focused revision materials with topics summarised for you in bite-sized chunks.

Read it!

Why?

Do you remember what we said about review? You should review material several times over to aid the memorising process.

Once you have created notes, the only way to review whilst actually using them is to read them.

If your notes have been made in the form of posters or flowcharts, then 'read' might in this instance mean 'look at'.

Tips

1 Read actively. This may mean reading out loud, or reading back and forth, flipping over pages, testing yourself.

2 On a similar theme, while you read the notes which you have prepared for yourself, make use of other resources available to you - use the quick quizzes given in the Study Text, for example, to test your memory of what you are reading, while you are reading it.

3 See if place association helps your revision:

Read through different sets of notes in different places, the bus, the library, the beach - see if you can build memory associations with the facts you are trying to remember. If you can think back to where you were when you were reading, your mind may find it easier to recall the facts that you were reading. Alternatively, if you use posters, where you put them will help to create a link - double entries for stock on the fridge, cash flow proforma above my bed, etc…

4 If you don't like reading, and feel that this stage is impossible - vary your review method. Tape your notes and then listen to them actively, in a similar way to that which is outlined above. Remember BPP's success tapes?…

> While revising, try **reading out loud**, even if it is not your usual custom. That way, you'll be **reading it**, and receiving the benefit of **hearing it**, too.

The review phase

The 'Read it!' phase is the key review phase of revision. You can review topics conveniently with BPP's passcards. You need to make the knowledge your own. It is up to you to look through whatever notes you have from stage 1.

You should try to vary this phase as much as you can - your mind likes things to be distinctive, and as you cannot vary what you are learning beyond the call of the syllabus, varying your method of review should add this element of distinction.

Teach it!

Tips

1 If you have kind people who are willing to help you in this situation, you might be advised to vary to whom you explain all the facets of your financial management course - even the best of friends can be put off by sustained exposure to technical detail!

2 Alternatively, you could genuinely use your guinea pig, or your rabbits, your cat, or your ted - while a real person may be able to challenge your understanding, in reality, they are probably not likely to, so it doesn't matter whether your pupil is animate or not!

3 Saying that, if you can carry out this phase with someone who is able to challenge your understanding - a study buddy perhaps? - so much the better. Become debating partners and you will be better equipped to approach the examiner's challenges.

Why?

Well, you're probably thinking 'that's your job!'. But bear in mind the motto of the French proverb quoted at the bottom of this page.

*Exams require you to **demonstrate** and sometimes **explain** your understanding. The best way to (1) practice, and (2) prove that you can do this is to include a phase in your revision where you 'teach' what you are learning to another person.*

Much of what you will learn is technical, and it may be that however well you explain it, without the basics, they cannot understand what you are talking about - do not let this dishearten you.

*This is a good way of **practising the skill of communicating your understanding**, which is a **vital link** in the exam chain.*

A french proverb

> "Teaching others teacheth yourself"

Do it!

Why?

We have already noted the importance of doing *question practice* as part of the learning process.

At the revision stage, bear in mind that the *reason* you are learning all these facts is *to answer questions* in the exam.

Practising questions will also help you practice important things such as exam *technique* (in relation to timing and such like) and *discipline* in your answers, which examiners comment time and time again, can make or break a candidate's script.

Another facet of 'do it!' is this: *if your paper is relevant* to a department that you work in, *use your work as an act of revision*. Consciously talk yourself through what you are doing and why as you go about your business - *justify your actions*, so to speak.

Tips

1 As part of your revision planning, you should timetable time to do questions.

2 Identify questions which you want to tackle at each stage of your revision, and then tick them off when they are done

3 At the revision phase, you should only really be attempting questions that are exam standard, unless you are still finding an area particularly hard.

4 As we said earlier, if you are running out of time in your revision phase, it is still worth using questions as part of your revision. If you do not have time to complete a full answer, try the following:

- Do an answer plan instead of a full answer.
- Attempt parts of a calculation

Exam focus

You are trying to pass an exam - that is your **key aim**. Try **imagining** what **questions** the examiner will ask - and think round **what the question is getting at**.

Question practice

BPP's Practice & Revision Kits contain lots of helpful **guidance** about questions - which to tackle and in what order. They highlight key questions, and contain a revision programme. You will find this helpful when it comes to question practice in your revision.

Remember also the kits also contain at least one mock exam. You should ensure that towards the end of your revision you attempt a mock exam in as near as full exam conditions as you can get, so that you are thoroughly practised.

Did you accept the challenge earlier in the chapter to list ways you can revise a topic quickly?

Here are our suggestions.

1 Read and summarise the chapter roundups and BPP passcards

To make sure you have taken in what you've read, try to **list** the ten **most important facts** or areas about the subject, or draft a quick **mindmap**.

2 Do the quick quiz

You can use the **quick quiz** to **identify gaps** in your knowledge where you need to refresh your memory. You may well find that removing these gaps pays dividends in the exam.

3 Do the MCQs

For papers containing MCQs, doing the MCQs **early** in your revision of an area can direct your attention to certain vital topics; you may have **struggled** with some of the MCQs or there may be facts and techniques that are tested as MCQs **over and over again**.

4 Audit the answer

WARNING! Auditing the answer can give **false reassurance**. Your belief that you would have come up with all the points that the answer contains may well be **false**. Nevertheless auditing the answer can provide some value, if you understand the **approach** the answer has taken. Also have a look at the **examiner's comments**, and think how you can ensure that you won't make the mistakes the examiner highlights.

5 Do an answer plan and/or attempt parts of the calculation

Going some way to **answer the question** is more valuable than just auditing the answer. Your brain will be more receptive to what the answer says if you have already spent a few minutes thinking about what you should do. You will also be **testing key skills**, tackling computations or structuring an answer.

Living through revision

Don't forget to live!

Finally, the best bit of advice that anyone doing revision can be given is 'don't forget to live.'

Sometimes people who are revising get so *uptight* and *worried* about the exams that they practically forget to breathe!

What did we say in Chapter 2 about relaxation? *A relaxed brain can take in knowledge - a tense one will not.*

As in all things we have mentioned, preparation is key. If you can *plan time off* into your revision period, then you will reap the dividends of an *alert* brain when you get back to study.

Of course, if you are rushed and trying to make up time all the time, you won't be able to get the relaxation you need.

Diet

Most importantly, remember to eat at all! Then remember to eat well - not quick snacks, but proper meals.

Sleep

It is vital that you sleep properly through your revision period so that your brain is rested. If you are having trouble sleeping, avoid working late into the night and try traditional methods, such as a glass of hot milk before you go to bed.

Enjoy yourself!

Lastly, enjoy yourself! We have highlighted the importance of taking time off. If you are taking time off, but spending that time thinking about the work that is sitting on your desk, then the time off is not worth anything. **If you take the time, really take it off!**

You may find that you experience the **association** phenomenon again - 'I remember revising all about the Stock Exchange in the morning on that day we went to Alton Towers in the afternoon…'

Types of question

- MCQs
- Scenarios
- Essays
- Numerical
- Other OTs
- Major case studies
- Law problems
- Report
- Discussion
- Financial analysis

Introduction

Content

Questions in exams take many different forms, and require answers ranging from a single letter, word or figure to a report requiring several hours to write.

However the main steps to follow are the same whatever the question. We explain what these stages are on these two pages, and go on to discuss in detail how to approach each type of question.

Remember!

Failure to answer the question set contributes to more exam failures than any other reason.

Remember!

The marks available for the question should determine the time you spend on it.

Focus on the requirements

The first step is to read and analyse the requirements of the question.

1 Instructions

The instructions will indicate whether the question is testing knowledge and understanding (explain, describe), application of knowledge (demonstrate, calculate), or analysis and evaluation (discuss, recommend).

2 Purpose

The purpose will determine the information you bring in and the techniques you should use. The recipient of your answer will be important in determining its purpose.

3 Scope

You need to identify specifically which aspect(s) of which subject area(s) are being examined.

Analyse the details

What you are looking for is the key information that will show you how to apply the question requirements and that you will use in your answer. This may include your role, business details and who will be reading your answer.

Some features recur regularly in certain types of questions. Question practice will enable you to spot these, and also help you identify traps set to distract you.

" Students are advised to focus on core topics of the syllabus and to practise past examination questions to ensure that they have an adequate grasp of the topics. "   *An examiner*

Which subject is the examiner talking about?

110

Plan your answer

Planning does not just involve writing down all the points you intend to make. It involves consideration of which points are the most important, also

- The structure of your answer
- The format of your answer
- The timing, how long each section of your answer should take and leaving time at the end to finish off

Check before you start that your plan makes sense, covers all relevant points and does not include irrelevant material.

Write your answer

Try to obtain all the easy marks you can before you move onto the difficult parts of a question. You may earn easy marks by writing out a proforma or slotting information from the question straight into your answer.

You can put a favourable slant on your answer by using clear English, short paragraphs, and underlined headings.

Finish off

You can gain crucial marks at the end of the time spent on a question by finishing off and tidying up your work.

- Total your calculations
- Draw conclusions or make recommendations
- Link main answer to appendices/workings
- Improve presentation (extra underlinings)

Features of a well-planned answer

▶ **Focused on key issues**

▶ **Good breadth**

▶ **Good depth**

▶ **Well-structured**

▶ **Points linked clearly**

▶ **Tidy presentation**

Writing your answer is much easier if you do a good plan.

The quote comes from the examiner's June 1999 report for CAT Paper C5 Managing Finances.

Unless you are a well-read C5 student, you are unlikely to have answered correctly; examiners for all types of subject have expressed similar sentiments.

Multiple choice questions (MCQs)

> **Multiple choice questions (MCQs)** are a popular means of testing knowledge and the ability to carry out basic calculations.
>
> In fact, they are a special type of objective test (OT) question. Other OTs are discussed in the next section. You will encounter MCQs and other OTs in computer-based assessments as well as on more conventional paper exams.
>
> They are often used to test breadth of knowledge; 20 MCQs can provide more balanced coverage of a syllabus than 3 or 4 longer questions.
>
> Past papers can give a good indication of what is likely to be tested within each topic area, and of areas of knowledge that are tested regularly.
>
> A
> B
> C
> D

Focus on the requirements

If you are doing your exam on paper (as opposed to on computer) you may prefer to read through all the questions first. You will then be able to see which questions you can answer easily, and which questions seem more difficult or will take longer to answer.

Generally question instructions will be straightforward, for example 'answer all the questions in Part A.'

The requirements will also contain instructions about how you should give your answer and what you should do if you change your mind. You should read these carefully; any answers that are ambiguous will be marked wrong.

Analyse the details

Although some MCQs will be straightforward, others may contain traps or irrelevant information.

You may find that some of a wording in a question seems familiar. If you think that you recognise it, you should nevertheless read the requirement and options carefully; do not assume the question is identical to one you have encountered before.

A warning

Time management is as important in tackling MCQs and other OTs as it is for more traditional questions.

Which one of the following is not a false statement?

    A   Charles Dickens was not an English novelist.

    B   Two plus two is not five.

    C   The Beatles came from New York.

    D   Peru, Bolivia, Paraguay and Tunisia are all countries in South America.

Plan your answer

Timing is an important decision; you need to decide how long on average you can allocate to each MCQ.

Even if MCQs represent x% of the marks, that does not always mean you should spend x% of the available time on them. Examiners sometimes expect that MCQs will be completed in a shorter time than suggested by their mark allocation.

Write your answer

Even if one of the options matches your own answer, be careful; the incorrect answers (distracters) are usually answers involving traps or common errors. You should make sure you take all relevant details into account and work through every stage of calculations.

You may find that none of the options matches your answer. If so, you should re-read the question, eliminate any obviously wrong answers and select whichever of the remaining options is the most likely to be correct. If you are still unsure, continue to the next question.

Finish off

Revisit unanswered questions. When you come back to a question you will often be able to answer it straightaway. If you are still unsure and are not penalised for incorrect answers, guess - never leave a question unanswered!

Timing

It is easy to run into time trouble if you are doing MCQs. The problem is that some MCQs can be answered instantly; others require working out. However by the end of your allotted time you should have an idea of whether you are near the answer to the MCQ or not. If you think you're nowhere near, leave the question. Note the question number against your rough workings and come back to it later, or just guess.

Wording

There are often many different MCQs that could be asked about the same piece of knowledge. The wording of some MCQs is therefore not straightforward. Not is often a key word in MCQs, as illustrated in the example on page 112, answered below.

Example of "verbal gymnastics" which can occur in an MCQ

The correct answer is B. The question is asking which of the statements is not false ie which of the statements is true.

A is false as Dickens was an English novelist, C is false as the Beatles did not come from New York. D is false as not all of the countries listed are in South America; Tunisia is in Africa. (If you answered D, thinking Tunisia was in South America, consider that the question asked for one answer; and 'two plus two is not five' is undoubtedly true.)

Other objective test questions (OTs)

> *Objective test questions (OTs) are questions that take various forms, but invariably require short, possibly single figure or word, answers.*
>
> *They have similar purposes to MCQs; a bank of OTs can be a very efficient way of examining a syllabus.*
>
> *Past papers can show you the types of OTs that are used and favourite topics for OTs. Be warned however that some examining bodies may introduce a greater variety of OTs, so it is essential to keep up-to-date with changes.*
>
> *OTs (including MCQs) are called objective test questions because they require little discretion or judgement on the part of the marker, who may even be a computer.*

Focus on the requirements

As with MCQs, you might wish firstly to look through all the OTs if you are taking a paper-based exam. This will help you see which questions are easy, and which seem harder or will take time to work out. You may on the other hand prefer to start at the front.

Because there are various types of OTs, you must ensure that you understand what the instructions say about the format of your answer. Markers will be trying to mark most OTs quickly; if your answer is ambiguous, it will be marked wrong. You need to identify whether you have to state an answer in words, or indicate it by ringing or deleting a word.

CIMA guidance on OTs

- ▶ Only answers will be marked, not workings nor justifications
- ▶ If you exceed a specified word limit, no marks will be awarded

You must therefore establish the limits placed on your answer. You may be asked to identify a single word, point, or a phrase. Definition questions may set a word limit that you cannot exceed.

Analyse the details

You may find that you recognise wording in a question when you sit the exam. If the question seems familiar read the requirement carefully - do not assume that it is identical, as the examiner may have inserted traps.

Fill in the blanks

Important elements in question requirements

……………, ……………, and ……………

Plan your answer

Some OTs can be answered instantly. However some will take time to answer, involving workings or careful consideration of what precisely you should write. You need to decide the timing of each question, bearing in mind the total time available and the mark allocation.

Write your answer

The key aspect of presentation is making the marker's life easier by avoiding alterations to your answer if possible. Therefore take care when writing the answer down.

> Because of the need for precision, and the difficulty of changing answers once written, you should consider doing some questions in rough first, for example definitions or diagrams.

If you are stuck at the end of the time that you have allocated to the question, you must move on to the next question.

Finish off

You should check to see that the answers you give are clear, and workings are not confused with answers.

For word limit questions, count the words to make sure you have stayed within the limits set. It may be possible to lose a couple of little words if you are a word or two over.

OT examples

CIMA has published the following list of possibles in addition to MCQs.

- ▶ *Filling in blanks in sentences*
- ▶ *Ranking items*
- ▶ *Stating a definition*
- ▶ *Identifying a key issue, term or figure*
- ▶ *Completing gaps in a set of data*
- ▶ *Identifying points/areas on graphs/diagrams*
- ▶ *Matching items*
- ▶ *True/false questions*
- ▶ *Writing brief explanations*

Examples of OTs in addition to MCQs are shown on the next two pages.

Important elements in question requirements

Instructions, Purpose and Scope

Objective test questions - some examples

1 Complete the following graph to depict a semi-variable cost.

£
Total
cost

Level of activity

2 An example of a semi-variable cost is

(Your answer must not exceed 10 words)

3 Fill in the gaps.

In a civil action the _____ sues the _____ . The burden of proof is _____ .

4 Is the following statement true or false?

The magistrates' courts deal only with criminal cases.   *TRUE/FALSE*

5 Which court or courts will normally deal with the following cases?

A claim for contractual damages of £21,000

A claim for tortious damages of £51,000

6 Sylvia pays no tax on the first £3,500 of her earnings and then

        22%   24%

        23%   25%

tax on the remainder of her earnings. She wishes to have gross earnings of £18,435 and wishes to have £15,000 net of tax earnings.

7   A mail order company has kept records of the value of orders received over a period. These are given in the following table.

Value of orders £	Number of orders
5 and under 15	36
15 and under 20	48
20 and under 25	53
25 and under 30	84
30 and under 35	126
35 and under 40	171
40 and under 45	155
45 and under 50	112
50 and under 55	70
55 and under 65	60
65 and under 85	54
	969

Class interval (value of orders) £	Frequency of orders	Height of block
$5 \leq 15$	36	A
$15 \leq 20$	48	B
$20 \leq 25$	53	C
$25 \leq 30$	84	D
$30 \leq 35$	126	E
$35 \leq 40$	171	F
$40 \leq 45$	155	G
$45 \leq 50$	112	H
$50 \leq 55$	70	I
$55 \leq 65$	60	J
$65 \leq 85$	54	K

Complete the table above by filling in the appropriate numerical value in the space indicated by the letters.

8   Fill in the gaps in the following sentence (one word for each gap).

Banks must _____ in order to make profits but part of their assets must be kept _____ if they are to meet depositors' requirements for withdrawals of _____.

117

Essays

Essay questions involve selecting and conveying information.

Examples

- ▶ Stating in detail
- ▶ Defining terms
- ▶ Describing key features
- ▶ Listing items
- ▶ Explaining the meaning
- ▶ Illustrating by example

Focus on the requirements

The instructions will determine the structure and depth of your essay.

Instructions such as 'list' indicate questions that are primarily tests of knowledge. Instructions such as 'explain' mean the questions are examining understanding as well. Questions testing understanding will require more consideration of underlying concepts and greater description than questions just testing knowledge.

Potentially the biggest pitfall with many essay questions is failure to understand their scope - remember they are testing your ability to select information. Examiners' reports often complain that answers consist of all candidates know about a topic area, and fail to focus on the specific aspects that the question is covering.

Analyse the details

If you are given extra details in the question, these will influence the content of your answer. If you have to describe key features, these will be features significant to the situation given in the question. If you are asked to illustrate by example, you will first look to use the information from the question.

"Describe the most important features of good accounts."

Why might you have problems answering that question as it stands?

Plan your answer

Most essays will need an introduction, main body, and conclusion, and should contain points that are clear and well-linked.

The criteria that you use to check whether your answer plan is complete will vary for each subject.

> In a law question, for example, you might ask whether your answer has covered all relevant types of law.

Check also:
- Every paragraph will contribute to answering the question
- No paragraph will be too long
- The answer will be in a logical order

Write your answer

If your answer has to cover a lot of points, you should keep reminding yourself to be careful of timing, and not to spend too long on each point.

The topic of each paragraph should be clearly visible. You can achieve this by giving each paragraph a header, and also by expressing the paragraph's main idea in the first sentence.

Bullet points, without explanation, are usually not enough.

Finish off

Your answer should contain a conclusion. This can refer back to the question or definition that started your answer, or it can highlight the most important points. However simply listing briefly the points you have already made in detail is unlikely to gain you any marks.

List questions

When you are asked to list a number of items, you should aim to give all items in the list.

The depth to which you discuss each item will depend on the time available and the importance of the item within the list.

Explanation questions

If you are asked to explain a concept unfamiliar to a layman, your answer should generally start with a short, simple definition of that concept.

Accounting is keeping financial records.

You then would go on to explain the general principles that relate to the concept. You should also consider whether there are any limitations or exceptions to the principles that you need to describe.

You are not told whether the question comes from a financial or management accounting paper, and your answer will depend on whether the accounts are to be used by the company's members and other stakeholders, or as internal management information.

Discussion

Discussion questions test your ability to think critically. Sometimes you will be given a framework for your discussion. On other occasions you will have to choose how best to **structure** your answer.

Types of discussion

- **Compare two subjects**
- **Discuss pros and cons**
- **Discuss for/against**
- **Discuss a proposition**

Propositions

Examples of propositions are whether X causes Y, how X impacts on Y, whether X is classified correctly.

Focus on the requirements

You should consider carefully the scope of your answer.

- The aspects of a subject area under discussion – unless you are told to the contrary, each key aspect will need equal treatment
- The opinions expressed in the question
- The words you will have to define or explain (for example if writing about benefits, why are they benefits)

The instructions may ask you to discuss, or may ask whether you agree with, a proposition. In both instances you will have to show why arguments that are contrary to your viewpoint are not convincing enough.

Analyse the details

The details in the question may indicate the various viewpoints you should consider. If you are not told, think about the various parties who might be involved in the discussion, and who might be interested recipients of your answer.

> Interested parties may include management, shareholders, debtholders or the government.

Remember also that you will need to approach the discussion from the perspective of the paper you are sitting. A discussion on an auditing paper would concentrate on implications for audits and auditors, a discussion on a financial accounting paper on the impact on statutory accounts.

> "Multiple choice questions are the best means of examining knowledge for lower level papers. Discuss"

Should your answer just cover multiple choice questions?

120

Plan your answer

Your answer should be structured around clear points, with the interrelationship between them highlighted. Your viewpoint will also influence your structure. You should therefore decide when planning your answer what your conclusion will be. Don't forget however to give due weight to views contrary to your intended conclusion.

An introductory paragraph may help set the discussion in context. However the detailed technical material you use in the body of your discussion needs to be selected carefully to support the points you are making.

> A common shortcoming in answers is excessive technical detail but little development of discussion.

You should check your plan before you start writing to confirm that you have covered all sides of the key issues fairly. Example plans for a discussion question are shown overleaf.

Write your answer

You need to be very careful when writing your answer with your timing, and avoid taking too long over single points or over one part.

Finishing off

You should draw a conclusion based on the previous paragraphs; you should not introduce new material that strengthens your argument. The conclusion should also indicate the key issues (the most significant arguments in favour of a proposition, or the most important differences between X and Y).

Proposition questions

- ▶ Introductory paragraph
- ▶ Each major point in, or implied by, proposition
- ▶ Significant arguments against proposition if not already covered
- ▶ Conclusion

Often the main arguments against a proposition will be counter-arguments to the points that support it.

Comparisons

- ▶ Introductory paragraph
- ▶ Point-by-point comparison
- ▶ Conclusion

If you are asked to compare X and Y, you should do so in each paragraph, rather than writing about X in the first half of your answer, Y in the second. Making a point-by-point comparison will help you bring out the main differences most clearly.

Although this proposition is about **multiple choice questions**, and your answer should concentrate on them, it also says that they are the **best** (not a good) way of examining knowledge. You therefore need to discuss whether any other methods might be better.

'It's a waste of time starting to study until a fortnight before the exam. Anything you learn before then you'll have forgotten by the time you come to take the exam.'

Do you agree?

Answer plan 1

Introduction

- ▶ Need to study for longer
- ▶ Can make study prior to previous fortnight effective

Is fortnight before long enough?

- ▶ Focus on essential knowledge/essential techniques
- ▶ Few do pass exams this way

But

- ▶ Syllabuses too large to be covered in fortnight
- ▶ Not enough time for effective question practice?
- ▶ Not time to get help
- ▶ Knowledge crammed in may not be remembered in exam

Study prior to fortnight

- ▶ Possible to remember for longer than fortnight
- ▶ Need to ensure regular recapping
- ▶ Use fortnight before for revision - practice key questions/reminder essential facts

Conclusion

Disagree - not long enough and can study effectively prior to fortnight

Answer plan 2

- **Long enough**
  - Key points
  - People do pass

- **Not long enough**
  - Can't cover syllabus
  - Can't practice questions
  - Can't get help
  - Crammed knowledge not remembered in exam

Fortnight

- **Longer than fortnight**
  - Can remember for longer
  - Fortnight before for essentials question/knowledge
  - Supplement by recapping

Law problems

Law problems are questions that give you the facts of a particular situation, and ask you about the legal position, or ask you to advise one of the parties. They test your ability to **apply** legal principles to specific situations.

Not all questions on law papers are problems. Often you will be merely asked to state or explain the law without any reference to a particular situation.

Focus on the requirements

The instructions may limit the scope of your answer to a certain area of law, for example consideration of civil (but not criminal) liability, or focusing on certain types of remedy.

If the purpose of your answer is to provide advice to a specific person, your answer should be written from the recipient's perspective, and should only include the issues that affect that person. If you are asked for a general analysis of the situation, you should cover all the main issues, even if certain issues do not affect everyone involved in the situation.

Analyse the details

The situation may well involve more than one legal issue, so make sure you read all the narrative thoroughly.

> The legal issues at stake will vary according to the area of law under discussion. In a criminal law problem, for example, you will be looking for the details that help you determine what crimes have been committed, and what the defences might be.

The legal issues to which you need to pay most attention are ones where there is uncertainty. There may be other points of law involved, but these may be unambiguous, and would warrant only a brief mention in your answer.

As you read through the question, you may identify that the circumstances of the case are similar to a case you have studied. You should note this down but be careful - the examiner might have introduced additional complications.

What should you do if you know that a legal principle was established in a certain case, but cannot think of the case name?

124

Plan your answer

There is a good general model for the structure of answers.

- Identify the legal issues involved in the scenario
- Explain the law
- Apply the law to the facts of the problem
- Conclude, supported by the rest of the answer

You should apply this framework differently depending on the area of law covered in the question. For example, in a contract law question you would discuss who can sue and be sued, on what grounds and with what consequences.

Remember that as well as explaining the law, it may be as important to state the limitations or exceptions to it.

Write your answer

You should concentrate on the principles expressed in relevant cases rather than the facts, and deal briefly, if at all, with issues of minor significance. You can improve the presentation of your answer by underlining statute references and case names.

Finish off

Don't forget the last part of the answer; you must draw a conclusion that is supported by what you have previously said. Don't let fear of reaching a wrong verdict prevent you from drawing a conclusion; remember that you can rarely be certain what the decision will be.

Pitfalls in law exams

"It is not enough for a candidate to conclude that the characters involved in the hypothetical dispute would be held guilty or not guilty without supporting argument. If it (were enough) candidates would have in effect a 50% chance of achieving a pass by guessing."

The quote is taken from an article by a CIMA law examiner. The article went on to list regular failings in law exams:

- Quoting cases and section numbers, but not providing any explanation.
- Writing a long list of rules hoping that one will be relevant.

If you can't think of a case name, don't worry too much. You will normally get credit for stating that the legal principle comes from a decided case, or identifying the case by highlighting its key details in a sentence.

Numerical

Numerical questions *are at the heart of many accountancy papers.*

Types of question

- *Filling in a proforma (set of accounts, cash budget)*
- *Carrying out a multi-stage calculation, for example a tax computation*
- *Carrying out a number of calculations, for example variance calculations*

For many questions, most of the marks will be available for doing the calculation, but some marks will be given for discussing what the calculation shows or the limitations of the method used.

In higher level papers, the calculations you carry out may be used as supporting evidence in a report.

Focus on the requirements

Even for simpler questions, you must follow instructions about what you are supposed to be calculating and what the scope of your answer should be (for example how many months should your cash budget cover?).

If the question does not specify what you should do, think about the purposes of your answer; what will your calculations show, and how will they be used by the recipient. The question details may give more information.

Analyse the details

Drawing a diagram may clarify question details, for example trying to illustrate the group structure in a financial accounting question.

You should look out for figures that are likely to need adjustment. If the information indicates that a figure should be adjusted, mark the figure on the question paper to indicate the adjustment that will be required. In a cash forecast for example, you may need to adjust sales for credit sales and cash received from previous periods' sales.

You should also try to identify irrelevant information or traps, for example details about non-cash items when you are asked to calculate cash movements.

Don't forget to look out for details that will help you answer the written parts of the question.

Give six examples of mathematical techniques other than addition, subtraction, multiplication and division that you will have to use regularly in accountancy exams.

Plan your answer

Think carefully about what calculations you should do.

- ▶ Can you use short cuts to avoid some of them?
- ▶ Can you do the easier calculations first?
- ▶ Which calculations are the most important?

You may be able to use a step-by-step approach to answer some questions. However the requirements may mean that you don't have to carry out all the possible steps.

The layout of your answer is also important. Not leaving enough room may seriously affect answer presentation.

You will need to decide whether you can do the written parts of questions first, or whether you will need to use the data from your calculations. A key element of timing is giving yourself enough time on the written parts, particularly in higher level papers.

Write your answer

You should try to avoid altering your calculations, as a large number of alterations will make your answer difficult to follow. A lot of the marks may be available for workings so make these clear. An example answer with supporting workings is shown on the next two pages.

Finish off

You should try to find time for some basic checks. These include trying to spot simple errors that hopefully can be corrected easily, also that figures in the main answer are cross-referenced to, and agree with, supporting workings.

A general approach

1 Easier marks

Initial simple calculations, writing out the proforma, putting numbers from the question into the proforma

2 Harder marks

More complicated calculations, calculations using the figures from the simple calculations, adjusting figures given in the question

3 Final stages

Doing the final calculations necessary to produce a result, totalling figures

4 Conclusion

Drawing a conclusion, is the balance sheet strong or weak, should the investment be undertaken, how should the currency risk be hedged etc.

We have listed some common examples below. If you are not comfortable with these, you must practice the techniques; a good business mathematics text will help you.

Calculating percentages and ratios

    Rounding

Approximation

    Manipulation of equations

Interest arithmetic, compounding and discounting

Presentation of data in graphs, charts, diagrams

    Calculating the mean and standard deviation

Use of index numbers

    Probabilities and use of the normal distribution

Panda Limited
Cash Budget for April to June

	Working	April £	May £	June £
Receipts				
Sales	1	2,700	34,020	103,680
Total receipts		2,700	34,020	103,680
Payments				
Materials	2		63,600	42,000
Labour	3	19,200	24,000	24,000
Variable costs	4		4,800	6,000
Fixed costs	5		12,000	12,000
New machinery			60,000	60,000
Total payments		19,200	164,400	144,000
Balance b/f		60,000	43,500	(86,880)
Net cash flow		(16,500)	(130,380)	(40,320)
Balance c/f		43,500	(86,880)	(127,200)

Workings

	April £	May £	June £	July £
1 Sales				
April sales (£27,000)	2,700	24,300		
May sales (£97,200)		9,720	87,480	
June sales (£162,000)			16,200	145,800
Total receipts	2,700	34,020	103,680	145,800
2 Materials				
April purchases (£30,000 + (40 x £840))		63,600		
May purchases (50 x £840)			42,000	
June purchases (50 x £840)				42,000
Total material costs		63,600	42,000	42,000
3 Labour				
April wages (40 x £480)	19,200			
May wages (50 x £480)		24,000		
June wages (50 x £480)			24,000	
Total labour costs	19,200	24,000	24,000	
4 Variable costs				
April (40 x £120)		4,800		
May (50 x £120)			6,000	
June (50 x £120)				6,000
Total variable costs		4,800	6,000	6,000

5 Fixed costs

£15,000 less £3,000 depreciation

Financial analysis

> **Financial analysis** involves using data to assess business performance, stability or prospects. Analysis is most often by comparisons with:
>
> ▶ Previous periods
> ▶ Budgets
> ▶ Other companies
> ▶ Expected or 'normal' levels
>
> Financial analysis is a useful tool at many stages, as a planning aid, as a means of obtaining evidence, or review mechanism.
>
> Financial analysis techniques are also important in other types of question, particularly *case studies* and *mini-cases*.

Focus on the requirements

You may be told which ratios you should calculate. Alternatively you may be asked to analyse the data to obtain evidence on important issues, such as recent performance or ability to pay debts.

Pay careful attention to what your analysis will need to discuss. Questions where you just have to carry out calculations are rare even in lower level papers.

> A very common complaint in examiners' reports is that analysis of calculations is insufficient or irrelevant.

Analyse the details

Key things to draw out from the information are:

1 Obvious changes. Have a general look at the figures first, to highlight the most significant areas.

2 Appropriate measures. Comparisons with previous years may not be of great use if there has been major additional investment.

3 Detailed measures. Total profits may be less important than profits for each location or per employee.

4 Reliability of information. Consider sources of information; are the company's figures reliable? This may require comment in your answer.

5 Significance of normal levels. Industry averages may be of little value if there is wide variation around them.

6 Likely reasons why figures might deviate. Look for business reasons that follow from the data you are given, not from wild speculation.

What are the main implications of the following figures?

	20X9	20X8
	£	£
Stocks	38,000	10,000
Debtors	16,000	14,000
Creditors	36,000	12,000

Plan your answer

If you are not told what ratios to calculate, you still need to be selective. Remember the purposes of the analysis, and:

▶ **Select the appropriate measures.** Firstly think which commonly-used comparisons may be relevant. Then think if there are any further measures that may also be significant.

▶ **Calculate a range of ratios.** If you have to choose what ratios to calculate, you should be choosing ratios that give different perspectives on the business. Your answer will lack breadth, for example, if you calculate four profitability ratios, but don't calculate any ratios relating to solvency.

▶ **Decide how far your written analysis should go.** As well as commenting on your calculations, you may need to discuss the limitations of what you have done. Limitations might include lack of data, manipulation of data, and significant non-financial factors.

Write your answer

You should make clear how you have carried out the calculations if there is more than one way of doing so, or what you have done is unusual.

You also need to structure your analysis in the most helpful way for the recipient. It may be best to put your commentary in the main answer, cross-referenced to an appendix containing detailed calculations.

Finish off

If the reader needs to take action, you should recommend what should be done, such as a company buying another company. Alternatively you may have to discuss how the business should remedy problems shown by the analysis.

Ratio analysis

Ratio analysis is particularly useful in assessing:

▶ *How the company has performed, what profits has it made*

▶ *How the company has managed stocks, debtors and creditors*

▶ *The possibility that the company may be in financial trouble*

$$\frac{X}{Y} = Z$$

You would concentrate on finding out the reasons why stock but not debtors has significantly increased (inability to sell stock perhaps), and whether the increase in creditors meant that the company had negotiated more favourable terms with its suppliers or had difficulty paying them.

Ratio analysis of stocks + debtors : creditors shows a figure of 2 in 20X8 and 1.5 in 20X9. This indicates that the assets provide less security than before for the amounts owed.

Reports

> **Reports** are very common in accountancy exams. For case studies and scenario questions your answer will most often be in the form of a report.
>
> We have included a separate section in this chapter on reports, as there are many features that will be common to all the reports you write.
>
> Sadly examiners' reports often comment on shortcomings in candidates' report writing skills.

Focus on the requirements

You need to note carefully what the instructions say about who the recipient of the report will be and the purpose for which it will be written.

Purposes of reports

- Assisting management
- Permanent record
- Provision of information
- Record of your own views

The recipient and purpose will influence:

- The content, what information is useful
- The form the report takes
- The language the report uses
- The explanations the report contains

A common failing of many reports (not just in accountancy exams) is that they are packed with jargon that the recipient does not understand, and information that the recipient does not need.

Analyse the details

Not all the information you are given in the question will be relevant. You need to concentrate on the information that will most influence your analysis and the recommendations you will be making.

You may need to make certain assumptions when writing your report. The assumptions you make should be realistic and should be stated clearly in the report.

How can you demonstrate quickly to the examiner that your report fulfils the requirements of the question?

Plan your answer

Your report must have a clear, logical structure. The key points should be emphasised, and discussed in depth. You should take care when selecting the points you intend to make; omitting details because they are contrary to your case may mean your report lacks objectivity.

You should also think about the best format for your report. This includes how you are going to use headings and spaces, and whether you need to include appendices.

We list opposite the details that a long formal report could contain. Shorter reports will not need every stage.

> An informal report may only need an introduction, a summary of findings and a conclusion.

Write your answer

When writing the report, you should be using objective and clear language. It may be better to use third person or impersonal language, rather than 'I' 'We'. As presentation is important, try to avoid crossing outs, alterations etc. Also keep an eye on timing, as your answer may be undermined if you have to omit points due to lack of time.

Finish off

Don't forget the recommendations if these are required. You should also check that all the 'signposts' in the report are clear, with points being cross-referenced to appendices.

Formalities

- Title
- Report writer
- Report recipient
- Date

Stages of a long report

- Contents
- Scope/terms of reference
- Information used
- Findings, in sections
- Summary
- Recommendations/conclusions
- Appendices

One good way of doing this is to use the question requirements as the heading for your report.

REPORT

To: Wendy Chan, Managing Director
From: Accountant
Subject: Analysis and recommendations regarding the proposed closure of the factory in Port Said and the move to Alexandria

Scenarios

*Typical **scenarios** are questions, often compulsory, that take at least an hour to answer and can range across all areas of a syllabus. They require you to show not only knowledge of the fundamentals of a subject, but also the ability to use the knowledge in a credible way in the context of a real business scenario.*

The distinction between scenarios and major case studies (described in the next section) is that scenarios are questions on a particular subject paper. Major case studies are sat as separate papers and require knowledge learnt for other papers at the same level.

Focus on the requirements

Sometimes very quickly reading the question details will give you a better idea of what the purpose of your answer is likely to be. However you should not start analysing the situation in detail before you know what you will be doing with the data.

The instructions may specify that your answer should be written for specific recipients. Your answer's scope will be influenced by why they want the information and their level of knowledge. The recipients may be implied by the paper and the instructions; for example a report on a client may be for an audit partner, but an audit programme may be for junior members of your audit team.

Analyse the details

You need to spend time familiarising yourself with the organisation described. This will mean, when you plan and write your answer, that you keep it focused on the scenario's subject.

When analysing the situation, you should look out for key factors that will influence your treatment of the problem, or the recommendations you make.

Possible key factors
- Size of organisation and hence the resources it has
- Factors influencing decisions
- Procedures and controls
- Weaknesses

There may also be paper-specific means of analysing the situation, for example using the balance sheet objectives as a means of assessing audit implications.

What is wrong with these recommendations for management

1 Choose a profitable segment.

2 Set a quantified objective.

Plan your answer

When you plan your answer, you may well find you have insufficient time to cover all the relevant issues in depth. This is because the *timing* is tight, testing your ability to *prioritise* and concentrate on the important issues.

Remember also that you may be expected to discuss the *limitations* of the techniques you use, or *other factors* you should take into account, even if you are not specifically asked to do so in the question.

The distinction between a scenario and a major case study (see page 136) may be relevant to the techniques you employ. For scenarios you may fall into the trap of using techniques that are too elaborate for the data you are given, or the amount of time you have to answer the question.

Write your answer

You should only bring in *relevant information* from the question, and do so succinctly; you should not be spending time copying out chunks of the question.

The *presentation* should be clear, in line with instructions and any answer layout preferences that the examiner has. You should not however spend excessive time on over-elaborating the appearance of your answer.

Finish off

You will probably have to offer a conclusion and *recommendations*. You should make sure that these are clear and specific.

> *Shorter scenario-type questions*
>
> *You may encounter shorter scenario-type questions. These are likely to be for fewer marks, and be restricted to certain areas of the syllabus. This sort of question will be a significant test of your technical knowledge. However it will also be testing your ability to:*
>
> ▶ *Select the right techniques*
> ▶ *Use the information given in the question*
>
> *to produce an answer that is **relevant** to the circumstances described in the question. You will often have to take into account the **size** of the client and the **nature** of the client's business.*
>
> *Answers to **all** scenario questions may have to be given in **formats** specific to the paper, for example in the form of an audit programme for auditing. You need to be confident with the **formats** that regularly occur in the paper.*

---

1 You should be giving the examiner specific advice on the criteria to be applied and the decision framework. If you have enough data, you should be making a recommendation yourself.

2 The advice is too general; you yourself need to take it (!), and say something like: 'I recommend that we seek to increase profits to £10 million by 2005. I believe this is achievable because customers will like the increase in product quality etc.'

Major case studies

Major case studies are separate papers typically requiring you to write a single report. You will often have to deal with an unstructured situation, and limited and ambiguous information.

Major case studies can examine a range of knowledge and techniques. Most importantly they test higher level skills.

- *Synthesis*, gathering data and getting the big picture
- *Analysis*, manipulation of data to find useful details
- *Evaluation* of data
- *Communication* in a form helpful to the user

You may receive all the information on the day of the exam. Alternatively you may receive a certain amount of information some time before the exam, and further information on the day.

Focus on the requirements

You may find it helpful to skim-read the information in the case study before considering the requirements. Do not however start analysing the situation before you understand all aspects of the requirements.

1 Instruction - generally to make recommendations for decisions

2 Purpose - consider the needs of the recipient, and how you in your role can help

3 Scope - determined by the decisions, the factors influencing decisions and the context (the business's internal and external, present and future situations)

Analyse the details

As you go through the data, you need to note or highlight clearly the information of great importance. This will be information that will have most impact on your recommendations, giving perspectives into the company's position, opportunities and challenges and possible courses of action.

You should also think about how you can manipulate the data to gain further insights, by using analysis techniques such as relevant ratio calculations, or what theories you might draw on in your answer.

> For case studies involving pre-seen material, the material you are given on the day will have a major impact on your answer. In particular, extra financial data will be highly relevant. You may therefore have to **modify significantly** your previous view of the organisation.

Your case study paper can tell the examiner more about you than any other paper. What do you think the following faults illustrate about the candidates' characters?

1 Failure to finish the question

2 Poor presentation

3 Lack of quantification in the form of objectives, budgets etc

4 Unconvincing arguments

5 Too much attention to the detail

Plan your answer

If you think the requirement falls into logical parts, structure your report round these. If the requirement is vague, you should identify the most helpful way of setting out your findings, for example separate discussion of timescales, markets and strategic business units.

You should also remember to prioritise relevant issues and write in most depth about the key ones; the timing will be tight.

Write your answer

Presentation is most important. You should start each section on a separate piece of paper. Each section and paragraph should be numbered in a hierarchy, to make cross-referencing easier.

> Appendices should include everything that the user does not need to know immediately to understand the contents of the report, such as matters of specialist relevance. You can also save yourself time by doing your calculations neatly, and putting them in an appendix.

Finish off

Your conclusions and recommendations (they are not the same!) should be in a separate section, backed by the arguments in your report. To ensure that your conclusions are supported by evidence, refer in them to the relevant paragraph numbers in your report. In addition your report may start with an executive summary. You should however write this last, as it summarises what you have done.

Pre-seens

Case studies where information is given out some weeks before are designed to get you to research the industry, type of firm, relevant theory and potential problems.

Tips

- ▶ Work steadily on the case throughout the period before the exam
- ▶ Don't get bogged down with small details in the case
- ▶ Research the case using the Internet, and also the press
- ▶ If you have identified the real-life business on which the case may be based, remember that the details you will be given on the day of the exam may differ from what happened in reality
- ▶ Don't confuse the further data you are given in practice case studies with the preseen data
- ▶ Don't try to prepare in advance one answer that fits all circumstances. Your answer must cover the extra data you are given on the day

---

1 Poor resource manager

2 Careless, unprofessional approach

3 Fear of financial aspects

4 Poor communicator

5 Lack of strategic overview

A marking matrix for a Case Study is shown on the next page.

Case study matrix

Most case studies are marked using a matrix that judges the answer according to a number of different criteria. The example matrix below is based on the marking guides used by the Chartered Institute of Management Accountants and the Institute of Chartered Accountants in England and Wales.

Possible criteria	Possible marks	Main elements
Knowledge	10	The knowledge used should be relevant and correct.
Numeracy and calculations	10	Calculations and workings should be correct. The right figures should be included in calculations. The written report should explain the results of calculations clearly.
Business awareness	20	The answer should identify the relevant business issues, demonstrate a critical approach and use real-life examples. Suggestions should be achievable.
Range of detail	10	The answer should include all the key issues and significant viewpoints. Assumptions should be criticised and limitations of data identified as appropriate.
Level of detail	10	The level of detail should be appropriate and arguments should be developed in depth.
Priorities	10	Most attention should be given to the most important points.
Format and structure	10	The answer should be in an appropriate format and in a logical order, with material subdivided and appendices used as required.
Conclusions and recommendations	10	Conclusions and recommendations should be valid and based on the content of the main report.
Business communication	10	The answer should be in a professional style with the necessary degree of formality. The main points should be expressed clearly. The answer should meet the audience's needs.
	100	

- Learning styles
- Types of subject
- Study environment
- Study skills
- Revision
- Types of question
- Exam paper

Exam paper

EXAM PAPER

ANY LEVEL

Any subject

ANY

INSTRUCTIONS TO CANDIDATES

> You are allowed as long as you like to read the material in this chapter, and you should refer back to it before taking any accountancy exams.
>
> Complete the checklists on the left-hand pages if you find them helpful. Answer all the quick quiz questions on the right-hand pages. Answers are at the end of the chapter.

Equipment requirements

	Night before	Day of exam
Pens	☐	☐
Pencils	☐	☐
Pencil sharpener	☐	☐
Rubber	☐	☐
Ruler	☐	☐
Geometrical instruments	☐	☐
Charting template	☐	☐
Calculator(s)	☐	☐
Spare batteries for calculators	☐	☐
Exam entrance documentation including candidate no.	☐	☐
Evidence of identity	☐	☐
Directions to exam centre	☐	☐
Watch	☐	☐
Handkerchief	☐	☐
Medication (hay fever, cough sweets etc)	☐	☐

The day before

Is last minute revision a good idea?

The most you should do is additional light revision of key points. Remind yourself of where you've made mistakes, so that you won't do the same in the exam. Revising topics for the first time just before the exam can crowd out the topics you have revised previously.

You also must try to rest. A good night's sleep the night before will do you far more good than last-minute, late night revision. It really does refresh the brain.

Equipment requirements

We list opposite items that you will need for most exams.

> You may need additional items for certain exams; do not forget to include these in your checklist.

If you can't sleep

If you think that you won't sleep the night before the exam, answer the quick quiz question below. If relaxation techniques don't work, you should nevertheless get into a resting position and make yourself comfortable.

Also don't worry. Doing the exam will provide you with the adrenalin you need to overcome any feelings of physical tiredness. Thinking to yourself that it will not matter if you can't sleep will actually relax you and help you nod off.

> Don't forget to set your alarm. It may be worth buying a second alarm clock, or an alarm clock that will not switch itself off.

Calculators

As well as taking spare batteries and/or a spare calculator, put new batteries in your main calculator and make sure it's working.

If you have a solar-powered calculator, remember that some exam halls are fairly dark, and your calculator may not work well under artificial light. You should consider taking a spare battery-powered calculator.

Quick quiz 1

Give three examples of relaxation exercises.

Travel arrangements

General

How much time will the journey take?

How much extra time will you allow yourself in case of any hold-ups?

Car

Are there any delays that you can find out about in advance?

Does your car have sufficient petrol, oil etc?

Do you know all details of the route? (The map that accompanies the exam instructions may only show the approach to the exam hall.)

What alternative routes can you use if roads are shut or traffic is too heavy?

Are there garages on your route that you could call into in an emergency?

Are you guaranteed a car parking space?

What will you do if your chosen car park is full?

Public transport (Train/Tram/Bus/Underground)

Have you used an up-to-date copy of the timetable to check running times?

Are there any delays that you can find out about in advance?

Do you know where you have to catch your transport?

Will you have to change transport during the journey?

How long have you allowed to make the connection?

For how long will you be delayed if you fail to make the connection?

Is there an alternative route you can use if there are delays/cancellations on your planned route?

Walk

What do you intend to do if the weather conditions are adverse (being soaking wet is not the best condition to take an exam)?

The day of the exam

What to eat

If you do normally eat breakfast you should certainly have a normal-sized, but not excessive, breakfast. If you don't normally eat first thing, consider nevertheless having something before the exam as it will increase your energy levels.

> It's best to avoid drinking excessive amounts of any liquid; you will not earn any marks during toilet breaks!

Directions

You should make sure in advance that you know the way to the exam hall. A practice journey shortly before the exam may help.

You must allow plenty of time to get to the exam hall. One possible rule is aim to arrive at the latest thirty minutes before the exam starts. You might allow more time if your journey is long or there is a risk of problems en route.

You should consult the radio or television travel news first thing in the morning, and just before you go, to check if there are any delays. These may mean that you have to use an alternative route.

> *If possible your practice journey should be at similar times to your actual journey. Travel conditions and timetables at the weekend may be very different to those you experience in the rush hour on the day of the exam.*

Once there

The only thing you should say about the exam to the other candidates is to wish them luck. You're better off discussing the state of the world, or how you plan to celebrate when the exams are over, than increasing each others' nerves.

Quick quiz 2

What can you do if you do arrive late for the exam?

Initial stages

Personal details

✓ Fill in your candidate number, centre details and other details on the front of your answer booklet.

Timing

✓ Check your watch with the clock in the exam room.
✓ Check how long you have to answer the paper, and write down the finishing time.

Format of paper

✓ Identify which questions are compulsory.
✓ Check whether you have to answer a certain number of questions from certain sections of the paper.
✓ Confirm how many optional questions you have to do.
✓ Ascertain the number of marks available for each question.

Reading through the exam paper

✓ Rank the optional questions based on the requirements of the **whole** question.
✓ Confirm that you are happy with the optional questions you have chosen.
✓ Write down the list of questions you intend to do and the order you intend to answer them.
✓ Confirm that your list includes **all** the compulsory questions and the **correct number** of **optional** questions.
✓ Allocate time to the questions in accordance with the number of marks available for each question, and allowing for time spent reading the paper and checking your answers at the end.

The start of the exam

Initial reactions

You may think that the paper is nowhere near as bad as you expected. You can answer all the questions and the only issue is how much you can write in the time available.

> Be careful! Adrenalin can be a very positive stimulus, but it can lead to excessive speed. If you rush at the start of the exam, you may choose the wrong questions or misunderstand what is being asked.

However you may feel that the paper is much harder than you ever thought it could be.

> But lots of others will be feeling the same! Everyone will have to do that difficult-looking compulsory question. You don't have to do that impossible optional question.

One way to limit the impact of your reactions is to spend the first few moments checking the timing and format of the paper. Completing these tasks will calm you down.

Reading through the paper

You must decide which questions to do, and the order in which you will do them. You may want to read through the paper twice to make the right choices.

As you are reading, you will find it useful to underline the key words in the question and jot down the most important points. This will help you decide which questions to do, and also aid your memory when you come to answer each question.

> *You will be sitting in the exam room for the next few hours. You won't achieve anything if you do nothing; you will achieve something if you pick up your pen and start writing.*

Quick quiz 3

What should you do . . .

(a) If a hot tip topic that you have revised thoroughly fails to appear on the paper?

(b) You are set a wholly written question on a topic that has previously only been examined by numerical questions?

Choosing questions

Criteria to use

Topics How comfortable you feel with the areas covered by the question will be a key influence on whether you choose it; but see below.

Requirements The requirements for some questions may be less onerous than others, requiring for example less depth of discussion. Whether requirements are broken down into parts or not may make the question easier to understand.

Scenario Consider how easy it will be to apply the requirements to the scenario you are given.

Easy marks It may be possible to gain a significant number of marks quickly before you tackle the difficult parts of the question.

Watch out for

Topics The question may be asking about an aspect of the topic you are less familiar with, or require greater depth of explanation than you have been expecting.

Topics (again!) The question may not just cover your favourite topics, but also include other topics that you like far less.

Requirements Beware of answering questions containing requirements that you are not sure you understand.

Unfamiliar terms Again be careful, but don't let unfamiliar terminology put you off doing the question if you are **sure** you know what it is asking.

Mass of detail Some questions will give a lot more detail than others. However it may be easy enough to work through the detail provided you adopt a logical approach. Indeed the main challenge in the question may be separating relevant detail from irrelevant, and once you have done that, the question will be straightforward.

Question selection

Choosing questions

You should read the questions carefully to ensure that you are choosing the best optional questions. We list opposite criteria you can use, and also indicate what can lead you to make the wrong decision.

> One way to choose questions is to grade each question and choose the questions with the highest grades. Alternatively you can try to work out quickly how many marks you think you can gain on each question.

Order of questions

You should also decide at the start of the exam the order in which you will tackle the questions. There are strong arguments for doing the question you think is easiest first. Starting with your best question will ease you into the exam and also increase your confidence when you attempt the more difficult questions later on.

> If the exam has MCQs or short answer questions, it is often best to do these first as you'll always be able to answer some of them, and no question will be that complex.

When you come to do certain questions, you may want to tackle the easier parts of the question first. If you answer a multi-part question out of sequence, check that the answers to the parts you answer first do not depend on the answers to the other parts. Also make sure that the marker can see clearly what you've done. Be warned however that many examiners dislike questions being answered out of sequence.

Before you start answering questions, it is worth having one further look through the optional questions, to confirm you are making the right choice.

1	Q5	9.50
2	Q6	10.30
3	Q2	11.10
4	Q1	11.50

Quick quiz 4

If the exam has a large compulsory question, for many more marks than any of the other questions, when should you attempt that question?

Doing questions

Focus on the requirements
- ✓ Skills and depth of understanding
- ✓ Purpose of answer
- ✓ Breadth of answer
- ✓ Marks available for each part of question

Analyse the details
- ✓ Key information
- ✓ Irrelevant material
- ✓ Traps
- ✓ Availability of easy marks
- ✓ Hints from the question on answer structure
- ✓ Overlap between areas covered by different parts of question

Plan your answer
- ✓ All necessary points included
- ✓ Points covered in sufficient detail
- ✓ Irrelevant material excluded
- ✓ Clear order and structure of answer
- ✓ Time allocated for answer reflects available marks

Write your answer
- ✓ Each point made contributes to answering question set
- ✓ Question number/part identified
- ✓ Handwriting and calculations clear
- ✓ Correct layout/format
- ✓ Paragraphs headed
- ✓ Paragraphs and sentences not too long
- ✓ Paragraphs well-structured
- ✓ Language appropriate (formality and technical content)
- ✓ No over-run on question timing

Finish off
- ✓ Calculations totalled
- ✓ Recommendations made and conclusions drawn
- ✓ Answer linked to workings/appendices

Check your answer (see later in this chapter)

Reading and planning

Adopting a disciplined approach

Be warned; you can lose a lot of marks if you rush in and forget what you've learnt about approaching questions.

Reading the question

Certain questions may strike you as familiar when you read the question paper. However it is very dangerous to assume that a question is identical. Answers may have been jumbled up on an otherwise identical MCQ. More complicated scenarios that seem on first glance to be the same will have different complications.

Planning your answers

You may find it helpful at the start of the exam to jot down the points we made about planning at the start of Chapter 6, to remind yourself of what you should do when planning your answer.

> Don't be put off by seeing people starting to scribble answers down straightaway. They will be throwing marks away by producing answers that are unfocused, unstructured and irrelevant.

Keep reminding yourself

You should remind yourself constantly whilst answering questions of the needs to present your answer well, to stay focused on the requirements of the question.

To avoid misinterpreting questions, you should read them thoroughly, and read them twice.

Quick quiz 5

Give two examples of verbs you might find in question requirements that test:

(a) Knowledge and understanding
(b) Application of knowledge
(c) Analysis and evaluation skills

151

An anti-checklist

Some students, if they are struggling with questions, try a number of strategies designed to confuse markers or enlist their sympathy. If you are tempted to try any of the list below, don't.

Markers are well aware of what students might attempt, and some of the tricks below may even cost you marks. For example, by writing down everything you know about a broad topic area, relevant or irrelevant, you may leave yourself insufficient time to develop the points that are relevant in sufficient detail.

What not to do

- ✗ Write over-lengthy introductions and conclusions whilst failing to develop the main body of your answer
- ✗ Provide uncalled for features such as situation analyses, executive summaries, background information
- ✗ Make endless assumptions or assumptions that transform what you have been asked to do into a different question
- ✗ Write what you want to say rather than what the examiner wants you to say
- ✗ Waffle!
- ✗ Write illegibly
- ✗ Provide an unclear structure hoping that the marker will get confused and give you the benefit of the doubt
- ✗ Use lots of technical jargon, write down whatever technical rules occur to you
- ✗ Pad out your answer by merely repeating the information given in the question and not using it to support your answer
- ✗ Tell the examiner what a hard life you've had and don't forget the good wishes for holidays etc.

Dealing with difficulties

Problems with questions

If the question appears difficult when you start answering it, jot down some ideas. Then ask what you need to do to fill in the gaps in your plan.

You may need to make assumptions to answer the question; your ability to come up with reasonable assumptions may be being tested. Your assumptions should be clearly stated at the start of your answer. However you must confirm before you begin writing your answer that your assumptions are reasonable and necessary.

> Read the question again to see whether there is information you missed on earlier readings which means that your assumptions are unnecessary. Also check that your assumptions are needed to answer the question.

Panic

If you find yourself getting stressed, pause briefly. Read the requirements again to confirm you are on the right track. If you are struggling with part of a calculation, remember what you are struggling with is only worth a few marks. Panic is normally not rational, just a manifestation of nerves.

Going back to questions

If you run out of time on a question, or feel you are stuck for now but might be able to say more if you come back to it later, leave plenty of space in your answer booklet and move on. If you do add extra points later on, make sure the answer's structure remains clear and the conclusion is apparent.

The assumptions you make may be a way of twisting the question away from what it actually asks, and towards what you would like it to ask.

Quick quiz 6

Why might the examiner be testing your ability to make assumptions?

Checking your paper

Exam details
✓ All necessary information on front of answer booklet is filled in.

Presentation and clarity
✓ Plan is clearly differentiated from main answer.
✓ Different parts of questions are labelled clearly.
✓ Formal documents (reports, letters etc) are headed correctly.
✓ Headers, underlinings are included if they are helpful.
✓ Final total or conclusion to answer is clearly shown.
✓ Where the answer ends is clear.
✓ Any work that you do not want the examiner to mark is crossed out.
✓ For MCQ papers, answer is clear and there are no other marks that could be read as answers. Also ensure that all MCQs have an answer.

Spelling and grammar
✓ Spelling and grammar are correct.
✓ Meaning of sentences is clear.

Arithmetic
✓ Arithmetic of answers is correct.

Workings
✓ Figures in main answer are cross-referenced to workings.
✓ Figures in main answer agree with workings.
✓ Main answer is clearly differentiated from workings.
✓ Arithmetic of workings is correct.

Appendices
✓ Main answer is appropriately cross-referenced to appendices.
✓ Main answer is clearly differentiated from appendices.

The end of the exam

Last question

When answering the last question, you may find you have one of two problems.

▶ You are struggling to come up with an answer. Rather than getting bogged down on one part, make sure you answer each part of the question.

▶ You are running short of time. The way to make the best use of the time is again to **obtain the easy marks first**.

For numerical questions this means writing out formats and entering quickly the simplest figures.
For written questions, you should produce a clear plan, make sure your answer has an introduction and conclusion and try to cover your best points.

Checking your work

For most papers it will be worth allocating a few minutes for **checks** that could gain or save you marks. If your checks identify problems that cannot be rectified in the time available (such as an arithmetic error in the first line of a long calculation question), add a note to your answer. Providing you have used the correct method in your answer, you should gain the necessary marks.

After the exam

As soon as you leave the exam, you should **forget about it** and concentrate on the next one, or if it is the last exam, celebrate! Don't discuss the paper with other candidates; there's nothing more you can do on it so why talk about it.

Don't let worrying about the exam affect your life. Lots of successful candidates reach the end of an exam sitting feeling they had at least one bad paper

Quick quiz 7

How can you avoid running short of time on the last question?

155

Answers to quick quiz

1
- Lying on the floor and relaxing your toes
- Lying in a bath with some relaxing music on
- Dancing away your frustrations

2 With most exams you should be allowed to take the paper provided you don't arrive too late. You will maximise your chances of passing if you attempt all parts of all questions, but let your time allocation for each part reflect the reduced time that you have available.

If you arrive too late to be allowed to sit the exam, you should still sit the remaining papers after the one you missed. Even if the exam board rule that you must take a group of papers together, they may allow you to take the paper you missed separately next sitting if your lateness was unavoidable.

3
(a) Forget about it! What isn't on the paper has no importance.
(b) Answer the question if it is compulsory; if the question is optional, don't let the fact that it is in an unusual format necessarily put you off answering it. It may still be easier than other optional questions.

If you feel a sense of injustice, bear in mind that the paper will be carefully analysed by tutors and the accountancy press, and the examiner will be made well aware of its shortcomings. Allowances will be made in the marking of problematic papers.

4 Very often the large compulsory question will be the most difficult question on the paper. If you do it first, and struggle, there is a risk that your confidence will be sapped for the rest of the paper.

You should consider doing it first if you feel it is reasonable, to put it behind you. Even if it appears difficult, you should avoid doing it last, and rushing it, as it is the most significant question on the paper.

5 Two examples from:
(a) Define, describe, distinguish, explain, identify, illustrate, list, outline, state, summarise, trace
(b) Apply, calculate, compute, demonstrate, prepare, produce, reconcile, solve, tabulate
(c) Advise, analyse, categorise, compare, consider, contrast, criticise, discuss, evaluate, interpret, justify, recommend, review

6 The assumptions you make may be a good test of your business awareness. For example if you are told that the business just employs the owner and a couple of other employees, you can assume that there will not be the types of elaborate controls that would be necessary in a large company. You can also assume that the finance available to the business will be limited (because of its size and circumstances, the business will not be seeking to raise money through the stock market in the near future, for example).

7
(a) Take the total time available for the examination.
(b) Subtract the time spent reading through the paper to select questions.
(c) Subtract the time allocated at the end for checking the answers.
(d) Take the remaining time and allocate it amongst the questions **according to the marks available for each question**.
(e) When you have decided the order in which you will do the questions, write down against each question the time when you should stop working on the question.
(f) When working on a question, and the time to stop arrives, move on to the next question.

Other books you might find helpful . . .

Acres D. (1998) *Passing Exams Without Anxiety.* (5th Ed). Oxford: How to Books Ltd — Good on revision

Buzan T. (1988) *Make the Most of Your Mind.* (2nd Ed). London: Pan Books

Buzan T. (1998) *Master your Memory.* (3rd Ed). London: BBC Worldwide Ltd — This is the book to read for detail on how mindmapping works etc ...

Buzan T. (1995) *The Mind Map Book.* (2nd Ed). London: BBC Worldwide Ltd

Buzan T. (1995) *Use your Head.* (4th Ed). London: BBC Worldwide Ltd — This book is helpful on reading and memory in particular

Chambers E. and Northedge A. (1997) *The Arts Good Study Guide.* (1st Ed). Milton Keynes: The Open University

Coman M. and Heavers K. (1998) *Improve your Study Skills.* (3rd Ed). Chicago: NTC Learningworks — This book is excellent! I would strongly recommend it as general book on study skills

Cottrell S. (1999) *The Study Skills Handbook.* (1st Ed). Hampshire: Macmillan Press Ltd

Drew S. and Bingham R. (1997) *The Student Skills Guide.* (1st Ed). Hampshire: Gower Publishing Ltd

Giles K. and Hedge N. (1995) *The Manager's Good Study Guide.* (2nd Ed). Milton Keynes: The Open University

Kemble B. (1980) *How to Pass Exams.* (1st Ed). London: Orbach & Chambers Ltd

McVea H. and Clumper P. (1996) *Learning Exam Skills.* (1st Ed). London: Blackstone Press Limited — This book deals with law specifically

Northedge A. (1990) *The Good Study Guide.* (1st Ed). Milton Keynes: The Open University — Good on essays

O'Brien D. (1995) *How to Pass Exams.* (1st Ed). London: Headline Book Publishing

Orr F. (1985) *How to Pass Exams.* (1st Ed). London: HarperCollinsPublishers

Race P. (1992) *500 Tips for Students.* (1st Ed). Oxford: Blackwell Publishers Ltd — Lots of bite sized tips to dip into

Rose C. and Goll L. (1992) *Accelerate your Learning.* (1st Ed). Aylesbury: Accelerated Learning Systems Ltd

Svantesson I. (1998) *Learning Maps and Memory Skills.* (2nd Ed). London: Kogan Page Ltd — Another useful look at mindmapping

Williams K. (1989) *Study Skills.* (1st Ed). Hampshire: The Macmillan Press Ltd — This book has a good section on notetaking

And . . .

BPP's courses and study materials are designed help you learn accountancy.